jerzy szapiro

the
newspaperman's
united
nations

a guide
for journalists
about the
united nations
and specialized
agencies

New York 1961
International Documents Service
a division of
Columbia University Press

By arrangement with the
United Nations Educational, Scientific
and Cultural Organization

*Published in 1961 by International Documents Service,
a division of Columbia University Press,
2960 Broadway, New York 27, N.Y.
Printed by Drukkerij Holland N.V., Amsterdam*

Preface

Since 1956, Unesco has been carrying out a programme for the improvement of facilities for the training of journalists throughout the world. As part of this programme, an International Centre for Higher Studies in Journalism was created at the University of Strasbourg (France) in 1957. More recently, in October 1959, a Latin America Centre was created at the Central University of Ecuador in Quito; and action along somewhat similar lines can be expected for South-East Asia and Africa.

As a further contribution to this programme, it was suggested that Unesco should sponsor the preparation of model handbooks for journalism teaching. It appeared to Unesco that the first textbook of this sort should best be devoted to the organization and activities of the United Nations and the Specialized Agencies. The author, Jerzy Szapiro, was asked to write a handbook on the United Nations family which could serve as a ready reference book and form the basis of courses on the subject for journalism schools. In the United Nations Secretariat, Mr. Szapiro filled the post of Director of External Services of the Department of Public Information in 1946–49, and was Director of the United Nations Information Centre at the European Office of the United Nations in Geneva from 1949 to 1956.

Attention is directed to the fact that, except where reference is made to membership lists and totals for the United Nations and for some other organizations (which have been updated to December or November, 1960), the data in this book reflect, unless otherwise stated, the situation as it existed at 1 January 1960. It will accordingly be realized that in addition to those mentioned some other changes, such as in the composition of committees or secretariats, have occurred since that date, and that furthermore no references have been made to later developments involving the United Nations in the Congo.

Contents

Introduction

The tasks and responsibilities of the United Nations and its Specialized Agencies now cover most of the field of human activity. The complexity of modern international organization leads to a great deal of confusion among the public; and it has never seemed more imperative that they should understand what the United Nations system is, what it does and how it functions.

It is the job of news personnel to present the peoples of the world with an objective, comprehensive, accurate picture of the work done by the various organs of the United Nations family and to help the public understand the processes by which the nations of the world promote their common interests and try to adjust their differences. Not the least part of their job is to dispel certain misconceptions concerning the role which the United Nations can play in world affairs, for these are the source of many disappointments, of indifference and even of cynicism. These misunderstandings are to a large extent due to expectations that the world organization will bring peace and prosperity in our time, and to the idea that the Charter of the United Nations was an instrument of radical changes in international relations. They also arise from the enthusiasm and zeal of many United Nations supporters, not matched by knowledge of the practices and methods—and the limitations—of an intergovernmental organization.

As early as 1947 the General Assembly of the United Nations became aware of the need 'to take measures at the earliest possible date to encourage the teaching of the United Nations Charter and the purposes and principles, the structure, background and activities of the United Nations'. In the course of its deliberations on freedom of information, the Economic and Social Council (Ecosoc) [1] of the United Nations at its

---

1. A list of abbreviations is given in Appendix VIII.

seventeenth session (held in New York in the spring of 1954), requested the Secretary General of the United Nations to prepare 'a concrete programme of action to promote among news personnel everywhere a wider knowledge of the work of the United Nations, of foreign countries and of international affairs, with a view to promoting friendly relations among nations based on the purposes and the principles of the Charter' —Ecosoc resolution 522 (XVII).

The resolution, 'recognizing the desirability of intensifying international action to assist in the professional training of information personnel', recommends action to this end by the member governments, by the United Nations itself, and by Unesco.

The present textbook may be regarded as a part of the programme to promote 'among news personnel everywhere a wider knowledge of the work of the United Nations'. It is primarily devised to be used in schools of journalism and in journalism training classes, to assist in teaching about the United Nations. It should also serve as a reference source for news personnel—that is, for editorial writers, accredited United Nations correspondents, radio and television commentators, and, in particular, editors and sub-editors handling United Nations news. It should help to guide them through the network of United Nations organs and their activities, assisting them in their daily routine dealings with United Nations material.

Those who use this book will find mention of a number of the more important publications in English on international organization, and should thus be able to discover supplementary material and comment on the policies, activities and achievements of the United Nations and its Specialized Agencies which this concise textbook could not provide, and indeed, was not intended to provide.

Course I

DEVELOPMENT OF INTERNATIONAL CO-OPERATION AND INTERNATIONAL ORGANIZATION: CREATION OF THE UNITED NATIONS

Man's efforts to secure peace and prosperity through union and co-operation of different tribes, cities, countries and finally of different nations, for common defence and the common good, are as old as history. Philosophers in ancient China taught mutual respect and co-operation in order to avoid war; the Achean League of Greek city states (368–146 B.C.) was an organized attempt at union in order to secure peace and welfare. The confederation of Swiss mountain cantons, differing in culture and religion and speaking four separate languages, has been in existence since 1291.

The demand for an international organization to prevent war has often been made in modern times. The French king Henri IV proposed a scheme for the political organization of Europe in his *Grand Dessein* of 1603; at the same time (1625) the father of international law, Hugo Grotius, wrote his *De jure belli ac pacis*, advocating, while Europe was being devastated by the Thirty Years War, international arbitration and conciliation for the promotion of peace.

In the 'age of enlightenment', Jean-Jacques Rousseau in his *Jugement sur la Paix Perpétuelle* (1761) proposed a confederation of 19 European States with a permanent Diet to settle disputes, outlaw recalcitrant States and proceed against them with combined forces. Immanuel Kant went further and proposed a world federation.

In the nineteenth century, under the impact of growing nationalism and scientific and technical discoveries, which led to modern indus-trialization and the speeding up of communications, statesmen and economists adopted the ideas of international co-operation and organiza-tion which had been propounded by philosophers and writers. The revolution in communications has now brought the most remote parts of the world nearer to each other than neighbouring towns were a hundred years ago. Much of the world's commerce has become international, and the interests of any one civilized country have become bound up with those of many other countries. The community of interests has extended to scientific and intellectual activity, which requires international collaboration in order to progress. Almost every public problem is now an international question: health, working conditions, nutrition, communication, trade, weather.

THE 'CONFERENCE SYSTEM'

After the Napoleonic wars the first serious attempt was made to establish an organized system of conducting international affairs with a view to preventing and avoiding war. At the Congress of Vienna in 1815 the 'Concert of Europe' was created by the four great powers of the period, Great Britain, Russia, Austria and Prussia, who decided to hold regular meetings to prevent future conflicts. This very inadequate 'conference system' of international organization, though lacking regular machinery to carry out its decisions and the participation of other countries—even when decisions directly affecting them were taken—nevertheless lasted a full century until the war of 1914. Two 'International Peace Conferences' held at The Hague in 1899 and 1907 tried to set up an international machinery for the prevention of war, based on larger co-operation. These conferences resulted in the Hague Conventions for the Pacific Settlement of International Disputes and in the creation of the Permanent Court of Arbitration, which still exists in the form of a panel of names of experts of international law from among whom arbitrators can be chosen.

The nineteenth century also saw the birth of international organizations dealing with non-political problems. These organizations were made necessary by industrial development and the extension of communications. They were the forerunners of the Specialized Agencies of the United Nations. The Universal Postal Union, created in 1874, and, in changed form, the International Telegraphic Union, are now members of the United Nations family of organizations. Some of these unions had permanent machinery which prepared their periodic conferences and carried out the decisions of the members—the prototype of an international secretariat—marking the transition from occasional conferences to international institutions.

The first world war caused an interruption in the development of the 'conference system'. It made clear the need for a universal system and an international machinery to settle international problems. The victorious allied nations of 1918 decided to create the League of Nations. Its Covenant formed an integral part of the peace treaty of Versailles.

THE LEAGUE OF NATIONS

With the creation of the League, the world entered the era of international organization, which was seen as a way of conducting international relations by means of permanent institutions to which member States assigned specific responsibilities and specific authority. The Covenant of the League, a multilateral agreement between signatories, specified these responsibilities as well as the obligations of the member States. It created the structure of the League, providing for an Assembly of all its member States meeting at regular intervals, and for a Council, composed of permanent members (the then great powers) and non-permanent ones, the member of which rose from four (as originally fixed in the Covenant) to eleven, with a permanent international secretariat.

The original permanent members were to be the principal Allied Powers—the United States of America, the United Kingdom, France, Italy and Japan—but the United States never became a member of the League. In 1926 Germany, and in 1934 the Union of Soviet Socialist Republics on joining the League, were given permanent seats in the Council. Subsequently Germany, Italy and Japan withdrew from the organization, thus reducing the number of permanent Council members to three. The League came formally into existence on 13 January 1920.

The Permanent Court of International Justice came into existence after its statute had been adopted by the League's Assembly.

The League was not able to prevent the second world war and could not survive it. It proved to be an imperfect instrument of peace. With its Covenant incorporated in the peace treaties, the League emerged from the Versailles Conference very much as a peace-time continuation of the victorious war-time co-operation of the great alliance, pledged to maintain the dearly-won peace. This was considered to be one of the major weaknesses of the League, and an attempt was made at its Assembly of 1938 to eliminate it by voting a resolution that the Covenant had 'an independent existence', and by passing amendments to the Covenant omitting all distinction between original members of the League and members subsequently admitted.

Based on the principle of sovereign equality of all member States, the Covenant went as far as to require a unanimous vote of all members in the League's Assembly and in its Council. This meant that every member had right of veto in the two principal organs of the League, contrary to the United Nations, where the rule of unanimity applies only to the vote of the permanent members of the Security Council. The powers of the League were strictly limited to recommendations: decisions to apply sanctions, when recommended by the Assembly or the Council, rested with individual member governments. The security system of the League was altogether much less elaborate and complete than that of the

Charter of the United Nations: no provision was made for armed forces to be placed by member States at the disposal of the League in its task of preventing war or suppressing acts of aggression. No specific provisions were made in the Covenant for organs in the economic and social field, and those subsequently created had no special status. Nor were provisions made for co-operation with the existing international specialized organizations.

PREPARATORY WORK FOR THE UNITED NATIONS

The experience of the League was drawn upon to a large extent in the establishment of the United Nations. In the first place, work on the Charter of the United Nations was begun while the second world war was still being fought: the special conference called for the purpose of drawing up the Charter met before the end of the war.

The basic principles of the future world organization were stated in the Inter-Allied Declaration, signed on 12 June 1941, at St. James's Palace in London, by the representatives of the governments of the United Kingdom, Canada, Australia, New Zealand and the Union of South Africa, and the governments in exile of Belgium, Czechoslovakia, Greece, Luxembourg, the Netherlands, Norway, Poland and Yugoslavia, and of General de Gaulle of France. 'The only true basis of enduring peace', said the declaration, 'is the willing co-operation of free peoples in a world in which, relieved of the menace of aggression, all may enjoy economic and social security. It is our intention to work together, and with other free peoples both in war and in peace, to this end'.

These aims were reiterated in the Atlantic Charter, proclaimed by President Roosevelt of the United States and Prime Minister Churchill of the United Kingdom on a warship in the Atlantic on 14 August 1941. They hoped to see established 'a peace which will afford to all nations the means of dwelling in safety within their own boundaries, and which will afford assurance that all the men on all the lands may live out their lives in freedom from fear and want'. The Atlantic Charter was later confirmed, on 1 January 1942, in the Declaration by United Nations at Washington which bore the signature of 26 nations, including the United States, the USSR and China.

The Moscow Declaration on General Security, of 30 October 1943, signed by representatives of the United States, the USSR, the United Kingdom and China, went a stage further. It said that the four governments 'recognize the necessity of establishing at the earliest practicable date a general international organization, based on the principle of the sovereign equality of all peace-loving States and open to membership by all such States, large and small, for the maintenance of international peace and security'.

The general outline of the Charter of the future organization of the United Nations was discussed at a conference in Moscow of foreign ministers of the 'Big Four' and in December 1943, at the meeting in Teheran of President Roosevelt and Prime Ministers Churchill and Stalin. The first draft of the Charter was prepared by representatives of the United Kingdom, the USSR and the United States at Dumbarton Oaks, a mansion in Washington, in August–September 1944. The proposals for the structure of the future United Nations were made public. Comments and criticism came from governments, from experts, and from members of the public of many countries.

The last stage in the preparatory work for drafting the Charter of the United Nations was the 'Big Three' meeting when Churchill, Roosevelt and Stalin met in Yalta in February 1945. A decision was taken on some of the most important questions left unsolved in the course of previous talks. As regards the voting procedure in the Security Council, the rule of unanimity of the permanent members was decided upon. It was also agreed to set up the international trusteeship system. On 11 February it was announced from Yalta: 'We are resolved upon the earliest establishment with our Allies of a general international organization to maintain peace and security.... We have agreed that a Conference of United Nations should be called to meet at San Francisco ... on the 25th April 1945 to prepare the Charter of such an organization, along the lines proposed in the informal conversations of Dumbarton Oaks.'

SAN FRANCISCO CONFERENCE

As decided in Yalta, delegates of 50 nations met at the Opera House of San Francisco for the largest international conference ever held, and sat for two months working on the Dumbarton Oaks draft and the Yalta agreement, which were considerably expanded and modified. The Charter is, in fact, more than twice as long as the Dumbarton Oaks proposals.

On 26 June 1945, the Charter of the United Nations and the Statute of the International Court of Justice were ready for signature by the 51 original members of the organization.[1]

The United Nations came into existence on 24 October 1945, when China, France, the United Kingdom, the USSR, the United States and a majority of other signatories deposited their instruments of ratification of the Charter.[2]

By a decision arrived at during the second session of the General

---

1. Poland signed the Charter on 15 October 1945 and thus became one of the original members although she did not attend the San Francisco Conference.
2. See list of Member States of the United Nations, page 197.

Assembly, 24 October is now observed as United Nations Day throughout the world.

The Preparatory Committee called to make provisional arrangements for the first session of the principal organs of the United Nations met in London, from 23 November to 23 December 1945. The committee consisted of one representative from each Member State, and its report provided the basis for subsequent decisions concerning the permanent organization of the United Nations, including the relations of the United Nations with the League of Nations, which was still formally in existence.

The first meeting of the first session of the General Assembly was held at the Central Hall in London, on 10 January 1946. The Security Council held its initial meeting on 18 January and the Economic and Social Council on 23 January. The International Court of Justice met for the first time in the Peace Palace of The Hague, on 3 April 1946. The Trusteeship Council was not constituted until after the Assembly met for the second part of its session in New York.

The League buildings in Geneva, including the Library, were transferred to the United Nations on 1 August 1946.

THE UNITED NATIONS:
WHAT IT IS AND WHAT IT IS NOT

The United Nations represents the latest stage so far reached in the history of international organization, in efforts to create a machinery by which nations work together for peace and for better living conditions for all mankind. The United Nations is *not* a world government and its General Assembly is *not* a world parliament, choosing and controlling a world administration. It is an agency to which member States assign specific responsibilities and specific authority under the Charter.

The Charter itself is a multilateral international agreement which specifies the obligations of Member States of the United Nations, defines the powers, the responsibilities, and the limitations of the organization and determines its structure and functions.

The organization's work of coping with problems of international relations is dependent on the will of the governments of Member States, in particular those of the principal powers. How well or how badly the United Nations functions depends on the degree to which its member governments co-operate and live up to their obligations under its Charter.

The machinery of the United Nations has proved suitable to its purposes whenever and wherever there has been a general will to use it to achieve these purposes. The common misapprehension about the United Nations is to see it as an organization which, overriding governments, can, independently of them, do the job of maintaining peace and furthering human progress. The most frequent mistake is to personify the United Nations: to blame the organization itself—and not the governments and the peoples who form it—for its shortcomings and failures. Friends and foes alike are guilty of such an attitude towards the United Nations.

AN APPRAISAL

For the past 15 years, representatives of national governments of the Member States have been meeting in the various organs of the United Nations and have been able to achieve a great deal in many fields of human activity. As Secretary General Dag Hammarskjöld said in the course of the tenth anniversary celebration in San Francisco: 'The influence of the Charter and institutions of the United Nations upon the course of events has been and will continue to be determined primarily by the governments. In their hand lies the power of decision. There have been many reasons —good ones and bad ones—why the United Nations has not yet become the focus of world efforts for peace in all the cases that its founders may have intended. . . . During all this time, however, a quiet process of construction has been going on. . . .

'On the basis of the Charter, international co-operation has been given an institutional framework and a continuity of programmes far more extensive than before in the history of nations. I speak not only of the United Nations, with its principal organs and commissions, but of the Specialized Agencies and other intergovernmental and non-governmental institutions related to it. This United Nations family of agencies with its thousands of international civil servants and experts enlisted from all over the world, is the main vehicle through which new traditions of working together for common purposes are beginning to be established among the nations, side by side with the older traditions of purely national service. . . .

'In this age of interdependence it is not possible for governments to serve many of their most vital national interests without taking into full account and giving due weight to the international interest. On the other side, what serves the true international interest also serves, whether in the short run or the long run, the true national interest. One of the chief purposes of the United Nations family of agencies should be to assist governments in their appraisal of the international interest and to be their instrument in thus serving the community of national interests.'

The future of the United Nations and the further success of international co-operation within the framework of a universal international organization—the United Nations system—will depend on the willingness of the governments to use the United Nations machinery, and on the determination of the peoples of the world to make the United Nations a success. The governments have their mandate from their peoples. The

Charter itself was written in the name of the peoples. Forty-two years ago, after the first world war, the peacemakers of Versailles, the authors of the Covenant, had written: 'The High Contracting Parties agree to this Covenant of the League of Nations. . . .' The Charter of the United Nations adopted at a public conference of 50 nations begins: 'We, the peoples of the United Nations . . . have resolved. . . .' This is not just a formula. It is a solemn pledge which imposes an obligation and a duty on the peoples of the world to use the democratic processes of government, nationally and internationally, to achieve the great aim of man 'to maintain international peace and security'.

BIBLIOGRAPHY

A bibliography of the Charter of the United Nations. New York, United Nations, 1955. 128 p.

BELL, Margaret; FELLOUGH, Hugh B. *International relations.* New York, Ronald Press Co., 1956. See Chapter 14.

CHASE, Eugene. *The United Nations in action.* New York, McGraw-Hill, 1950.

CLAUDE, Inis L. *Swords into ploughshares; the problems and progress of international organization.* New York, Random House, 1956.

Everyman's United Nations, 1944–58. Sixth edition. New York, Department of Public Information of the United Nations, 1959.

FENICHELL, S. S. *The United Nations: design for peace.* New York, Holt, Rinehart & Winston, 1960. 144 p.

GOODRICH, Leland M.; HAMBRO, Edvard. *Charter of the United Nations: commentary and documents.* Boston, World Peace Foundation, 1946. 413 p.

HADWEN, John G.; KAUFMAN, Johan. *How United Nations decisions are made.* Leyden, 1960. 144 p.

HARLEY, John Eugene. *Documentary textbook of the United Nations.* Second edition (revised). Los Angeles, Center of International Understanding, 1950. 1470 p.

HILL, Norman. *International organization.* New York, Harper, 1952.

How it all began. New York, United Nations Department of Public Information Research Section, no date.

LEONARD, Larry. *International organization.* New York, McGraw-Hill, 1951. See Chapters 2 and 3.

LEVI, Werner. *Fundamentals of world organization.* Minneapolis, University of Minnesota Press, 1950.

MacLAURIN, John. *The United Nations and power politics.* London, Allen & Unwin, 1951.

SCHWARZENBERGER, Georg. *Power politics: a study of international society.* London, Institute of World Affairs, 1951. See Chapter 15.

The Charter of the UN and the Covenant of the League of Nations. New York, United Nations Department of Public Information Research Section, no date.

United Nations Conference on International Organization, San Francisco, 1945. Documents. London, New York, United Nations Information Organization, 1945. Volumes 1 to 3.

VANDENBOSCH, Amry; HOGAN, W. N. *The United Nations: background, organization, functions, activities.* New York, McGraw-Hill, 1952. 456 p. See Chapter 3.

WALTERS, F. P. *A History of the League of Nations.* London, Oxford University Press, 1952. 833 p. See Part I.

WORTLEY, B. A. (ed.). *The United Nations: the first ten years.* Manchester, Manchester University Press, 1957. 206 p.

Yearbook of the United Nations, 1959. New York, Office of Public Information, United Nations, 1959. 660 p.; and previous editions, starting with 1947.

Course II

THE GENERAL ASSEMBLY
OF THE UNITED NATIONS

On the third Tuesday of September, the annual forum of world affairs begins in New York, in mid-Manhattan. The General Assembly of the United Nations meets for its regular session.

The Assembly, according to the Charter, 'may discuss any question or any matter within the scope of the . . . Charter or relating to the powers and functions of any organ provided for in the Charter', and may make recommendations 'to the members of the United Nations or to the Security Council or to both on any such questions or matters' (Article 10).

It is the one organ of the United Nations in which all Member States—99 of them now—are represented. Each delegation may send five delegates, five alternate delegates and as many advisers and counsellors as it deems necessary. The Councils of the United Nations—the Security Council, the Economic and Social Council, and the Trusteeship Council —submit their reports for consideration by the Assembly. So does the Secretary General, who not only reviews the work of all the organs of the United Nations, but also states his views on the international situation at the time of writing his report.

These reports are submitted to Member States, together with a provisional agenda, 60 days before the opening of the session. They are made public. The budget estimates for the next year are also circulated at the same time, together with financial reports of the preceding year. Member governments have the right to submit proposals for additions to the provisional agenda.

When the annual session of the Assembly opens, the head of the delegation which provided the President of the preceding session takes his seat on the dais, with the Secretary General on his right and the Executive Assistant to the Secretary General on his left. He faces the semi-circle of the delegations in the big Assembly Hall of the United Nations buildings.

All the meetings of the Assembly are open. Galleries are set apart for the general public and for the press. All seats—for the delegations, press, and public—are provided with earphones for listening in to simultaneous interpretation of everything that is said in the Assembly from the President's dais and from the speaker's rostrum. The official languages are: Chinese, English, French, Russian and Spanish. A statement made in any one of these languages is simultaneously rendered in the four other languages by interpreters who work in booths looking on-to the Assembly Hall.

CONSTITUTION OF THE ASSEMBLY

The session is opened by the Temporary President. His inaugural speech usually contains a review of the current political situation and of the part played by the United Nations in world events for the past year. The election of the President is the first business of the Assembly. No names are submitted. The President is elected by simple majority, each delegation recording one vote. The ballot is secret. The Assembly has already evolved a routine in respect of the presidency of the Assembly. It is not given to the big powers, and representatives of large regions or groups of States are elected in rotation. The delegations usually agree beforehand on the name of the candidate, and the choice rarely comes to a close vote.

The election of the President is followed by that of 13 Vice-Presidents of whom five are chosen from the delegations of the permanent members of the Security Council.

After the nomination of a Credentials Committee of nine members, the Assembly adjourns to allow its main committees to be constituted and their officers to be elected. These committees consider agenda items referred to them by the Assembly and prepare recommendations for the final vote by the Assembly. They are:

First Committee, Political and Security;
Special Political Committee;
Second Committee, Economic and Financial;
Third Committee, Social, Humanitarian and Cultural;
Fourth Committee, Trusteeship, Non-self-governing Territories;
Fifth Committee, Administrative and Budgetary;
Sixth Committee, Legal.

The chairmen of these committees, together with the Vice-Presidents, form the General Committee which is headed by the President of the Assembly. This committee deals with the organization and the conduct of business of the Assembly—e.g., it considers all requests for new items to be placed on the agenda.

After adopting the agenda for the session, the Assembly begins the general debate in which the heads of the delgations usually express the views of their countries on problems of common concern to the membership of the United Nations.

THE ASSEMBLY RECOMMENDS

The General Assembly of the United Nations is not a legislative international body. It cannot impose its decisions on the Member States; its action takes the form of recommendations. However, as the main deliberative organ of the United Nations, the General Assembly is in a central position in the organization, for it has the right to discuss and make recommendations on all matters within the scope of the United Nations Charter; it has the right to discuss the powers and functions of the other United Nations organs, which submit annual reports to it; and it considers and approves the budget for the entire organization. Furthermore, all 99 member nations of the United Nations are represented in the General Assembly.

Each member nation has one vote, and every vote is equal. Important questions—such as recommendations regarding the maintenance of international peace and security, the election of members of United Nations Councils, questions of membership of the United Nations, matters relative to the operation of the trusteeship system, and budgetary questions—are decided by a two-thirds majority of the members present and voting. Other questions are decided by a simple majority, including the determination of what other specific decisions are to be taken by a two-thirds vote. Unlike the situation which obtained in the League of Nations the rule of unanimity, even of the great powers, does not apply to the General Assembly.

Ideas developed by delegates in the course of debates may not directly affect the voting, but can and do affect public opinion in various countries and through it the policies of the governments.

The General Assembly meets regularly once a year. It had originally been expected that the regular sessions of the Assembly would last no longer than the four weeks which was the maximum in the League of Nations Assemblies, but the average duration of a session is now ten to twelve weeks. A special session may be held if the Security Council or a majority of the members wants one. An emergency special session may also be called, on 24 hours' notice if necessary, to consider any apparent threat to the peace, breach of the peace or act of aggression on which the Security Council, because of a veto, has been unable to take action. In such a case, the Assembly may recommend collective measures, including the use of armed force. An emergency special session may be requested by the Security Council on the vote of any seven members or by a majority of the members of the United Nations. Two special sessions, on the question of Palestine, and three emergency special sessions, two on the Middle East and one on Hungary, have been held.

FUNCTIONS AND POWERS

The Assembly initiates studies and makes recommendations aimed at promoting international co-operation in the political field and encouraging the progressive development of international law and its codification; and at promoting international co-operation in the economic, social, cultural, educational and health fields, and assisting in the realization of human rights and fundamental freedoms for all without distinction as to race, sex, language or religion.

Problems are brought before the Assembly by Member States and by other United Nations bodies. A non-member State may bring to the attention of the Assembly any dispute to which it is a party if it accepts in advance, for the purposes of the dispute, the Charter obligations of pacific settlement.

The Assembly may discuss any international problem brought before it and may recommend what should be done, except, however, that, when the Security Council is acting on a matter affecting peace and security, the Assembly may not make any recommendation unless the Council asks it to do so. The Assembly has the power to adopt recommendations only, not binding decisions; the force of such recommendations is that they represent the judgement of the majority of the 99 United Nations member nations.

Electoral functions form an important part of the work of the Assembly. It chooses, by a two-thirds majority of those present and voting, the six non-permanent members of the Security Council, the 18 members of the Economic and Social Council (Ecosoc), and elective members of the Trusteeship Council. Each year three members of the Security Council and six members of Ecosoc are nominated—the first for two years, the second for three years. By simultaneous but separate balloting the Assembly and the Security Council, independently of each other, elect the judges of the International Court of Justice. The Assembly also appoints the Secretary General of the organization on the recommendation of the Security Council. It admits new member nations to the United Nations when they are recommended by the Security Council.

SUBSIDIARY BODIES OF THE GENERAL ASSEMBLY

The organs of the Assembly are of two kinds, those functioning during the session only, like the main committees, and various standing bodies, which deal with continuing problems.

Two of these standing committees are provided for in the Assembly's rules of procedure: the Advisory Committee on Administrative and Budgetary Questions (composed of nine members) and the Committee on Contributions (10 members). The other standing bodies established by the Assembly are: the Board of Auditors (three members), the Investments Committee (three members), and the United Nations Staff Pension Committee (nine members).

All five of these committees deal with administrative and financial questions and the titles indicate their functions.

The Assembly has at various sessions appointed a number of committees and offices for special purposes. Of those still functioning mention should be made of: the United Nations Commission for the Unification and Rehabilitation of Korea, the United Nations Conciliation Commission for Palestine, the United Nations Relief and Works Agency for Palestine Refugees in the Near East, the Office of the High Commissioner for Refugees, the Committee on Information from Non-self-governing Territories, and the Collective Measures Committee.

Subsidiary to the Assembly is the permanent International Law Commission. Another subsidiary body is the Peace Observation Commission.

The Assembly also established a subsidiary organ which could function between the Assembly's regular sessions. This body, the Interim Committee, popularly known as the 'Little Assembly', was created in 1947 for one year, extended for another year in 1948 and re-established for an indefinite period in 1949. In recent years, the Interim Committee has met only once at the beginning of the year to elect officers. Establishment of the Committee was regarded by Byelorussia, Czechoslovakia, Poland, the Ukraine and the USSR as contrary to the Charter and they never attended any of its meetings.

UNITED NATIONS MEMBERSHIP

The original United Nations membership of 51 in 1945 had grown to 99 by October 1960. The membership was then as follows:

Afghanistan	Burma	Chile
Albania	Byelorussian SSR	China
Argentina	Cambodia	Colombia
Australia	Cameroun	Congo (capital:
Austria	Canada	Brazzaville)
Belgium	Central African	Congo (capital:
Bolivia	Republic	Léopoldville)
Brazil	Ceylon	Costa Rica
Bulgaria	Chad	Cuba

Cyprus	Ivory Coast	Portugal
Czechoslovakia	Japan	Rumania
Dahomey	Jordan	Saudi Arabia
Denmark	Laos	Senegal
Dominican Republic	Lebanon	Somalia
Ecuador	Liberia	Spain
El Salvador	Libya	Sudan
Ethiopia	Luxembourg	Sweden
Finland	Madagascar	Thailand
France	Malaya, Federation of	Togo
Gabon	Mali	Tunisia
Ghana	Mexico	Turkey
Greece	Morocco	Ukrainian SSR
Guatemala	Nepal	Union of South Africa
Guinea	Netherlands	Upper Volta
Haiti	New Zealand	Union of Soviet
Honduras	Nicaragua	Socialist Republics
Hungary	Niger	United Arab Republic
Iceland	Nigeria	United Kingdom
India	Norway	United States of
Indonesia	Pakistan	America
Iran	Panama	Uruguay
Iraq	Paraguay	Venezuela
Ireland	Peru	Yemen
Israel	Philippines	Yugoslavia
Italy	Poland	

BIBLIOGRAPHY

Annual reports of the Secretary General on the work of the organization. These form a part of the official records of the General Assembly.

Rules of procedure of the General Assembly, 1956. Document 1.8.

Course III

POLITICAL QUESTIONS

PART I

World events of the last few years and their repercussions in the United Nations have thrown a most illuminating light on the place the United Nations occupies in world politics, on its possibilities and limitations.

In November 1956, the hopes and the confidence of the peoples of the world, alarmed and disturbed by the Suez Canal crisis and by events in Hungary, turned to the United Nations, which became the focus of international politics during those fateful weeks. News from the Manhattan building was spread over the front pages of papers in the remotest corners of the globe.

A year later, in a changed atmosphere, in a period of calm expectation, the General Assembly, at its twelfth session, did its job without drama, with little publicity, with hardly a mention in the press of its deliberations, except for a few days of rather artificial crisis.

In 1958, again, the thirteenth session was preceded by an emergency special Assembly to take cognizance of a successful pacifying action of the United Nations in the Middle East, which contributed largely to ending a dangerous conflict between some Arab States.

The United Nations mirrors the realities of the world situation. It does this now more truly than ever before because, with the increase of its membership, it is approaching universality. In the critical autumn of 1956 the majority of United Nations Member States, including some of the big powers, had a vital interest in using the United Nations as an instrument for negotiations and for concerted action: hence vital decisions were made, such as creating the United Nations Emergency Force, and placing strong pressure on the parties involved in the conflict to accept the Assembly's verdict. In the autumn of 1957 the tendency was to mark time. Negotiations outside the United Nations were the principal object of certain powers who, even in problems such as disarmament which are strictly and specifically of United Nations competence, made their attitude depend on the results of these negotiations. In 1958, again, an important task was imposed on the United Nations—and completed with success—because the organization was thought to be the best instrument for restoring calm in the Middle East.

The interest in 1956, the indifference in 1957, the renewed interest next year, were all reactions of the public to the debates and the decisions of the General Assembly. In the evolution of the Assembly's and the Security Council's functions and relationship, the shift towards the Assembly was marked with particular clarity in those three years.

THE SECURITY COUNCIL

The Security Council is one of the six main organs of the United Nations. The others are: the General Assembly, the Economic and Social Council, the Trusteeship Council, the International Court of Justice and the Secretariat.

The task of the Security Council is to promote the establishment and the maintenance of international peace and security in all parts of the world.

Members of the United Nations, in giving the Security Council the main responsibility for keeping the peace, have agreed that in carrying out this responsibility the Council is acting for them all.

The Council has eleven members. Five of these (China, France, the USSR, the United Kingdom and the United States) are permanent members. Six others are elected by the General Assembly for two-year terms.

Each member of the Council has one vote. On procedural matters—such as adoption of the agenda—decisions are made by the affirmative vote of any seven members. On all questions not of a procedural nature, the required seven affirmative votes must include the votes of the five permanent members. A negative vote by any permanent member means rejection of the proposal or resolution on which the Council is voting. This is what is sometimes called the 'veto power' of the permanent members. In practice, the Council does not regard a permanent member's abstention from voting as a 'veto'.

Any United Nations member, not a member of the Council, may participate, without the right to vote, in any discussion of the Council, if the Council considers that the interest of that member is affected. Any State, whether a member of the United Nations or not, which is a party to the dispute being considered by the Council, may be invited to participate, without vote, in the discussions.

The Council holds itself in readiness to meet at any time whenever peace is threatened. For this purpose, each member of the Council is represented at all times at United Nations Headquarters.

Pacific settlement of disputes.   The powers and functions of the Council are specified in Chapters VI–VIII and XII of the Charter. The Council may investigate any dispute or situation which might constitute a danger to the peace. Such a dispute or situation may be brought to the attention of the Council by any member of the United Nations (and also by any non-member, if it accepts in advance the obligations of pacific settlement under the Charter), by the General Assembly, by the Secretary General who is authorized to bring to the attention of the Council any matter which he thinks may threaten the maintenance of the peace. The Council recommends methods of adjusting such disputes or suggests terms of settlement.

The Council determines the existence of a threat to peace, a breach of the peace, or an act of aggression and it has the power to take prompt action and decide on enforcement measures to maintain or to restore peace.

Enforcement action not involving the use of military force may consist of calling on members to interrupt economic relations, to cut communications or to sever diplomatic relations. Should these measures prove inadequate, the Council may take military action by air, sea or land. It may decide on demonstrations, blockade, or any other operation by forces of the members of the United Nations.

United Nations members have undertaken to make available to the Council armed forces, assistance and facilities, including the right of passage necessary for the maintenance of peace. The Military Staff Committee, a permanent subsidiary body of the Council, consisting of representatives of the Chiefs of Staff of the permanent members of the Council, was deputed to plan the application of armed force (i.e., immediate and effective military action under United Nations auspices) in the event of a crisis. In April 1947 the committee presented a report on the general principles of organizing armed forces, but could not agree as to the over-all strength and composition of the forces to be placed at the disposal of the Council. It also failed to agree on how to study other aspects of the matter, and has held no further discussions since August 1948. The committee formally exists—it changes its chairman each month, etc.—but it does not in fact function. It had no part in the organization of the United Nations Command in Korea or in the creation of the United Nations Emergency Force in the Middle East.

Besides maintaining international peace and security, which is its principal task, the powers of the Security Council extend to other fields, as follows: It decides whether a State is qualified for membership of the United Nations, before the Assembly (on the Council's recommendation) can vote its admission; it is also empowered to recommend to the Assembly the suspension of the rights of any member, against which it is taking preventive action, or the expulsion of a member which persistently violates the principles of the Charter. The Council has never as yet exercised these powers.

The Council is responsible for all functions of the United Nations under the trusteeship system with regard to those territories which are classified as 'strategic areas'.

The Secretary General is appointed by the Assembly on the recommendation of the Security Council.

THE VETO PROBLEM

As early as the second part of the first session of the Assembly, in 1946, concern was voiced by many delegations as to the effects of the veto clause on the work of the Council. In 1948 the Assembly recommended that the permanent members of the Council should seek agreement among themselves upon what decisions they might forbear to exercise the veto, when seven affirmative votes had already been cast in the Council. No agreement was reached by the permanent members.

The Assembly's recurring debates on the veto, and its fruitless recommendations, echoed the criticism of the veto system voiced in many parts of the world. This is not the place to go into the merits of the dispute about the veto, but it should be stressed that the veto was introduced into the Charter at the insistence of the big powers, and that it applies to a limited—though most important—part of the activity of the United Nations. No veto exists in other Councils, in the General Assembly, or in the Specialized Agencies.

To enable the General Assembly to perform more effectively the functions entrusted to it by the Charter in the field of international peace and security and particularly in situations in which the Security Council was unable to act because of the veto, the Assembly adopted in November 1950, three resolutions under the title 'Uniting for Peace'.

These resolutions provided for special emergency sessions of the Assembly at 24 hours' notice, on the vote of any seven members of the Security Council or a majority of United Nations members, in a case where the Security Council, because of lack of unanimity among the permanent members, failed to act in respect of a breach of the peace, a threat to the peace, or an act of aggression. It also established a Peace Observation Commission of 14 members (including the five permanent members of the Security Council) to observe and report on the situation in any area where international tension threatened peace and security, and a Collective Measures Committee of 14 to study methods to be used collectively to maintain and strengthen peace and security.

The machinery established in the 'Uniting for Peace' resolutions was used in the emergency of October–November 1956, in connexion with the Suez Canal and the Hungarian crises. There was compliance with the Assembly's resolution calling for the withdrawal of foreign troops from Egypt, but not in the case of Hungary. Constitutionally, under the Charter, only the Security Council has the power to *order* the use of force and to take action to implement its decision. In the case of recommendations of the Assembly, the decision to implement these rests with the respective member governments.

The Collective Measures Committee, which the USSR declared illegal and in which it refused to participate, presented a report on 'methods which might be used to maintain and strengthen international peace and security'. It suggested denunciation of the offending State, its suspension or expulsion from the United Nations and non-recognition of changes brought about by the threat of use of force. Economic sanctions would involve severance of trade and financial relations, embargoes, etc. The report also dealt with the organization and utilization of a United Nations military force. The Assembly, in 1951, noting the report with approval, asked the committee to pursue such studies as it might deem desirable. The committee has not done any further work since.

DISARMAMENT

The Charter has singled out disarmament and the regulation of armaments among the 'general principles of co-operation in the maintenance of international peace and security' which guide the United Nations. It charged the United Nations to elaborate principles of disarmament and to formulate plans for establishing a system for regulating armaments (Article 26).

At its first session the Assembly established the Atomic Energy Commission to seek means of eliminating atomic weapons and other weapons of mass destruction, and to promote the use of atomic energy for peaceful purposes. In 1947 a Commission for Conventional Armaments was set up. In view of the very limited progress of these two bodies, a single Disarmament Commission was formed in 1952 to take over the functions of the other two bodies. The commission consisted of all the members of the Security Council and of Canada.

However, the commission was also unable to report progress, and in 1952 the Assembly suggested the creation of a small subcommittee of the powers who were principally involved to seek (in private meetings) an acceptable solution. The subcommittee—consisting of Canada, France, the United Kingdom, the United States and the USSR—met in London in the spring of 1954. For the sake of brevity (and of clarity) we shall confine the review of the disarmament debates in the United Nations to the period beginning with the creation of the subcommittee.

THE TWO BASIC PLANS

In June 1954, France and the United Kingdom submitted a proposal for a disarmament programme which would at the beginning prohibit the use of nuclear weapons, and later provide for prohibiting the manufacture of such weapons, for a major reduction of armed forces and conventional armaments, and for the creation of a control organ to supervise the observance of a disarmament convention.

The USSR at the Assembly of 1954 accepted these proposals as a basis for future negotiations and proposed that in the first year there should be simultaneous reduction of armaments and military expenditure by 50 per cent from the 1953 level, to be supervised by an international control commission. In the second stage a further reduction would take place, with a simultaneous prohibition of the production and the use of all mass destruction weapons, this to be supervised by a control body with the right of inspection.

In subsequent debates, when both sides presented more detailed versions of their proposals, essential differences appeared. The Western powers insisted upon a drastic reduction in the armed forces and conventional armaments of the great powers *before* complete prohibition and elimination of nuclear weapons and the institution of an effective system of control. The USSR insisted on an immediate complete prohibition of nuclear weapons, *simultaneously* with a reduction of conventional forces. States possessing military, naval and air bases in the territories of other States, were to liquidate them.

In 1955 the subcommittee adjourned to await the outcome of the Geneva meeting, in July of that year, of the heads of government of France, the United Kingdom, the United States and the USSR. The views expressed at that meeting were forwarded to the subcommittee, which simply reported to its parent body, the Disarmament Commission, which in turn sent the report to the Assembly.

The Assembly, at its 1955 session, suggested to the subcommittee that, in its endeavours to reach an agreement on a comprehensive disarmament plan, it give priority to such 'confidence-building measures' as President Eisenhower's Geneva plan for exchange of military blueprints and aerial inspection, and Marshal Bulganin's plan for control points at strategic centres, as well as other feasible measures of adequately safeguarded disarmament.

Seven members headed by the USSR voted against the resolution. In the debate the Soviet representative maintained that the Western powers were proposing control without disarmament, and were trying to substitute talks on the gathering of information on arms instead of giving consideration to ending the armaments race and prohibiting nuclear weapons. The representatives of the Western powers pointed out that the problem of control was the cardinal point. The work on disarmament must be based on the principle 'no control taken separately without disarmament, no disarmament without control'; progressively, all such disarmament as can be currently controlled.

THE 'PARTIAL MEASURES' PLAN

In the summer of 1957, six partial measures were proposed in the sub-committee by its four Western members as a first step to disarmament, but these were rejected by the USSR. The essentials of the six-point plan were subsequently included in the Assembly resolution on disarmament (November 1957) which suggested a disarmament agreement providing for:
1. Immediately suspending nuclear weapons tests, with effective international control.
2. Ceasing production of material for nuclear weapons and using all production of fissionable material for peaceful purposes, under effective international control.
3. Reducing stocks of nuclear weapons under international supervision.
4. Reducing armed forces and armaments through adequately safeguarded arrangements.
5. Progressively establishing open inspection with ground and aerial components to guard against the possibility of surprise attacks.
6. Study of an inspection system to ensure that the sending of objects through outer space would be exclusively for peaceful and scientific purposes.

The resolution was approved by a majority of 57 to 9 with 15 abstentions. The representative of the USSR thought that the partial measures would not in any way inhibit the armament race; they did not prohibit the use of nuclear weapons, which the Western powers utilize as the principal element in their policy of positions of strength. The USSR voted against the resolution.

TOWARDS THE CESSATION OF NUCLEAR WEAPONS TESTS

However, through diplomatic channels and exchanges of notes, an agreement was reached by the three 'atomic powers', the United States, the United Kingdom and the USSR to take action on the first point of the resolution—that of suppressing the testing of nuclear weapons. It was decided first to convene a meeting 'of experts to study the possibility of detecting the violation of a possible agreement on the suspension of nuclear tests', and, on the basis of the report of the technicians, to work out a draft of an international convention.

As a result of the agreement between the three 'atomic powers', experts from the United States, the United Kingdom and France, on one side, and the USSR, Poland and Czechoslovakia on the other, met in Geneva in the summer of 1958, the United Nations providing all the necessary conference facilities under the direction of a special representative of the Secretary General. On 21 August, the experts—atomic scientists and nuclear physicists of the highest standing—agreed unanimously on a report which was submitted to their respective governments.

It contained an analysis of the various methods of detecting nuclear explosions, and suggestions for a central control system for observing an agreement to prohibit the tests. A conference of high level officials then met to prepare the draft of a convention on the cessation of nuclear tests for subsequent approval by a conference of ministers. The officials met in Geneva on 31 October 1958, and were still in session at the beginning of 1960 trying to find compromise solutions for a few problems still remaining to be settled.

CONFERENCE ON SURPRISE ATTACKS

To study the technical aspects of measures against the possibility of surprise attacks, experts met in Geneva in November 1958 and adjourned *sine die* after a six weeks' debate on the agenda and procedure, without being able to agree as to the subjects to be discussed. Eight countries participated: the United States, the United Kingdom, France and Italy on the Western side, and the USSR, Poland, Rumania and Czechoslovakia on the Eastern side.

The opening statements by the leaders of the two groups marked the differences. The spokesman of the Western powers described the task of the conference as being 'to analyse the technical facts which bear upon the problem of the possibility of surprise attacks', to provide a basis for future political considerations of the subject. The spokesman of the Eastern group was of the opinion that 'reliable measures for prevention of an attack can be worked out only on the condition of a complete prohibition of atomic and hydrogen weapons . . . the liquidation of military bases on foreign territory and a substantial reduction of conventional weapons and armed forces'.

The efforts to bridge the gap between the technical and the political approach to the problem bore no fruit, and the conference decided to adjourn and to report to governments who would decide on the date of reassembly.

ATOMS FOR PEACE

One of the main items of the disarmament debate in the United Nations was the prohibition of the use of nuclear weapons and the utilization of

37

nuclear energy for peaceful purposes. While no agreement has as yet been reached on any problem concerning nuclear weapons, the creation of the International Atomic Energy Agency (IAEA) [1] crowned the efforts of the United Nations to organize international action for the peaceful uses of atomic energy.

A scientific committee on the effects of atomic radiation had been set up in 1955 to gather information on radiation effects on man and his environment, with the co-operation of the International Atomic Energy Agency, the World Health Organization and the International Labour Organisation. The first report of the committee, sent to the Assembly in 1958, dealt with the effects of ionizing radiation. The Assembly asked the committee to continue its useful work.

The two great conferences on the peaceful uses of atomic energy organized by the United Nations in 1955 and 1958, contributed to the world-wide exchange of information and knowledge on the progress of atomic science and techniques.

THE PEACEFUL USE OF OUTER SPACE

Following the launching of artificial earth satellites by the USSR and the United States, these two powers requested the United Nations to consider this problem. The Assembly, 'conscious that . . . developments in respect of outer space have added a new dimension to man's existence and opened new possibilities for the increase of his knowledge and the improvement of his life', decided in 1959 to establish a 24-member committee to deal with questions of research and mutual exchange of information about progress in this field, and with legal problems which may arise in using outer space.

THE COMMITTEE OF TEN

In September 1959, the delegations of France, the USSR, the United Kingdom and the United States transmitted to the United Nations the text of a communiqué issued in the name of the foreign ministers of the four powers. The communiqué said that at the Foreign Ministers' Conference in Geneva, they had discussed the possible means by which further negotiations on the question of disarmament could be most effectively advanced, and had reached agreement on the setting up of a Committee of Ten on disarmament (composed of Bulgaria, Canada, Czechoslovakia, France, Italy, Poland, Rumania, the United Kingdom, the United States and the USSR).

In the communiqué, they noted that 'ultimate responsibility for

1. For details on IAEA, see Course XIII.

general disarmament measures rests with the United Nations' and said that the setting up of the new committee 'in no way diminishes or encroaches upon the United Nations' responsibilities in this field'. Rather, it was intended to take account of 'the special responsibility resting on the great powers to find a basis for agreement'.

'The four governments,' said the communiqué, 'conceive of this committee as a useful means of exploring through mutual consultations avenues of possible progress toward such agreements and recommendations on the limitation and reduction of all types of armaments and armed forces under effective international control as may, in the first instance, be of particular relevance to the countries participating in these deliberations. Furthermore, it is the hope of the four governments that the results achieved in these deliberations will provide a useful basis for the consideration of disarmament in the United Nations.'

The United Nations Disarmament Commission, meeting a few days later, adopted a resolution welcoming the planned resumption of consultations on disarmament. The commission also welcomed the declared intention of the countries concerned to keep it appropriately informed of the progress of their deliberations, and expressed hope that the results achieved would provide a useful basis for the consideration of disarmament in the United Nations. The resolution was adopted unanimously.

In November, the General Assembly adopted, also unanimously, a resolution noting 'with approval' the Disarmament Commission's report on the matter.

Two of the six resolutions adopted by the General Assembly during its 1959 disarmament debates specifically referred matters to the 10-nation committee.

One—the unanimously sponsored and unanimously adopted resolution on the item 'general and complete disarmament'—transmitted to the new body 'for thorough consideration' the declarations made by the United Kingdom and the USSR on 17 and 18 September respectively, and also all other proposals and suggestions put forward during the Assembly debate on the matter. The United Kingdom's declaration outlined a three-stage disarmament plan. The declaration of the USSR contained a four-year programme for general and complete disarmament.

The other resolution dealt with the problem of preventing the wider dissemination of nuclear weapons. It suggested that the 10-nation committee 'consider appropriate means whereby this danger may be averted, including the feasibility of an international agreement, subject to inspection and control, whereby the powers producing nuclear weapons would refrain from handing over the control of such weapons to any nation not possessing them and whereby the powers not possessing such weapons would refrain from manufacturing them'.

The vote in favour of the resolution was 70 to 0, with 12 abstentions (Albania, Bulgaria, Byelorussia, China, Czechoslovakia, France, Hungary, Peru, Poland, Rumania, the Ukraine and the USSR).

PART II

The preceding course described the United Nations machinery for dealing with political problems, the working of this machinery and the functions of the Security Council and the General Assembly in this field.

Information is given in the present course on some political problems and cases dealt with by the United Nations. In making the selection the author has been guided by topical interest—that is by the fact that the problems are actually on the United Nations agenda—and by the relative importance of the issues. Account has also been taken of the fact that the cases are characteristic of methods of action used by the organs of the United Nations and of endeavours to meet, in the best way possible, obligations under the Charter. It is not intended to list the numerous decisions and recommendations in the field of international politics which have been made by the United Nations in the past 15 years. This explains certain omissions, even of actions which are justly, and universally, regarded as undeniable achievements of the world organization.

MIDDLE EASTERN PROBLEMS

The Palestine question.   Palestine has been a permanent item on the political agenda of the United Nations since a special session of the General Assembly, in May 1947, established a committee on Palestine under British mandate. This committee, after a thorough study of the problem, presented a plan for the partition of Palestine into an Arab and a Jewish State, with Jerusalem under international régime, all three units being linked in an economic union.

The plan, approved by the Assembly in November 1947, was accepted by the Jewish Agency, but was rejected by the Arab High Committee, which advocated the establishment of an Arab State, with a guaranty of protection for the Jewish minority.

The situation in Palestine steadily deteriorated and another special session of the Assembly was called on 16 April 1948. It decided to appoint a United Nations mediator for Palestine to promote a peaceful adjustment between Arabs and Jews and to assure the protection of the holy places. Count Folke Bernadotte, the President of the Swedish Red Cross, was named mediator.

Creation of the Jewish State: the Arab-Jewish war.   The decisions were taken by the Assembly on 14 May 1948, and the special session adjourned. On the same day the United Kingdom mandate over Palestine expired. A Jewish State was proclaimed under the name of Israel.

The next day the Arab States embarked upon an armed action against the new State. A four weeks' truce, imposed by the Security Council on 11 June, was not extended due to the refusal of the Arab States. The war continued despite the efforts of the mediator and repeated orders of the Security Council to cease military action. On 17 September, the mediator, Count Bernadotte, was shot dead in the Israeli sector of Jerusalem. Ralph Bunche of the United Nations Secretariat was appointed acting-mediator. He succeeded in bringing about a cease-fire on all fronts in January 1949.

Egypt and Israel signed a General Armistice Agreement at Rhodes on 24 February 1949, followed by similar agreements between Israel and Lebanon, Israel and Jordan and Israel and Syria. The agreements set up mixed armistice commissions to supervise their implementation. A three-member Conciliation Commission was named to assist in achieving a settlement of outstanding questions. In August 1949, the Security Council urged the parties to negotiate a final peace settlement, either directly or through the Conciliation Commission.

The difficult task of supervising the armistice agreements is performed by the United Nations Truce Supervision Organization (UNTSO), an international group of military observers headed by a Chief of Staff, who is also the Chairman of the four Mixed Armistice Commissions which deal with the complaints of the parties.

The Security Council has been frequently called on to liquidate recurring clashes, to consider numerous complaints of violence and aggression from one or the other party to the armistice agreements.

In October 1956, the Council was once more convened to deal with an emergency situation on the complaints of both Jordan and Israel. At a meeting on 25 October, the Israel representative declared that his government did not attach importance to 'routines of verbal condemnations and investigations' which had not been able to make the life of a single Israeli safer. Israel was prepared to observe the cease-fire agreement as long as it was observed by the other side.

Israel marches on Egypt.   Five days later, the Council met urgently at the request of the United States which informed it that armed forces of Israel had penetrated deeply into Egyptian territory in violation of the armistice agreement. The Egyptian delegate stated that this unprovoked attack constituted an act of war. The representative of Israel retorted that Israel had taken security measures in self-defence against groups from Egypt which had been invading Israeli territory.

The following day, the United Kingdom delegate informed the Council that the United Kingdom and French governments had called upon both Israel and Egypt to stop all warlike action and withdraw their forces to 10 miles from the Suez Canal. The Egyptian Government was asked to agree that Anglo-French forces should move temporarily into key positions at Port Said, Ismailia and Suez to protect free passage through the Canal. Twelve hours were given for compliance with the request, otherwise the British and French forces would intervene to secure compliance.

The Suez Canal problem, arising out of the nationalization of the Suez Canal Company by Egypt, and brought before the United Nations after direct negotiations had failed to produce a solution, had thus become linked with the Palestine question in the most acute crisis the United Nations had had to face since the outbreak of the Korean war in 1950.

The Suez Canal question. This came before the United Nations after an unsuccessful effort had been made by a group of users of the Canal to establish an international system which would guarantee the use of the Suez Canal at all times and by all powers. Egypt rejected international control of any kind over the Canal. The Security Council, at the end of September, outlined six requirements for the Suez Canal: free and open transit for shipping, respect of Egyptian sovereignty, the operation of the Canal to be insulated from the politics of any country, tolls and charges to be decided in agreement between the users and Egypt, a fair proportion of dues to be allotted to development, and disputes to be settled in arbitration. These were adopted unanimously.

The Secretary General entered into negotiations with the Egyptian Government for arrangements to meet these requirements, when military action in the Canal zone turned the attention of the United Nations to the more urgent task of the cessation of military operations in the Suez Canal and Sinai area.

The Security Council met on the evening of 30 October to consider, before the time limit of the Franco-British request expired, Egypt's demand that action be taken to prevent the act of aggression involved in the threat of force and imminent occupation of Egyptian territory. A resolution of the United States calling for Israel to withdraw behind the armistice line and for all United Nations members to refrain from the use of force in the area, was not adopted, France and the United Kingdom voting against. When the Council resumed discussions next afternoon, it was faced with news of attacks by French and British aircraft against military targets in Egypt. The Suez Canal was subsequently blocked, when Egypt sank ships and bridges, and closed the Canal to navigation.

The Security Council being unable to take a decision owing to the veto of France and the United Kingdom, an emergency special session of the Assembly was called. Next day by an overwhelming majority, the Assembly adopted a United States resolution calling for an immediate cease-fire, withdrawal of armed forces, a scrupulous observance of the Palestine Armistice Agreement, reopening of the Canal, and restoration of freedom of navigation. The parties involved accepted the resolution with various reservations, which necessitated further elucidation, thus delaying the cease-fire.

Creation of the United Nations Emergency Force: cease-fire. The turning-point came on 3 November, when, on a proposal by Canada, the Secretary General was instructed, by a vote of 57 to 0 with 19 abstentions, to set up an emergency international United Nations force to secure and supervise the cessation of hostilities. General Burns, the Chief of Staff of UNTSO, was appointed commander of the United Nations Emergency Force (UNEF) and organized his staff. The United Kingdom and France approved the idea of interposing a United Nations force between Israel and Egypt, and of fixing a cease-fire under United Nations terms. On 5 November Israel informed the Secretary General that all fighting had ceased. The cease-fire by the United Kingdom and French troops took effect at midnight 6–7 November, after the forces had occupied Port Said and Port Fuad. The withdrawal of Israeli and Anglo-French forces was to begin with the arrival of the United Nations Emergency Force.

The United Nations force—units from 10 countries—began to arrive by plane in the Canal zone on 15 November. In February 1957 it was brought to its full complement of some 6,000 men and officers, following the withdrawal of Anglo-French forces which was completed on 26 December 1956, and then moved to positions along the Egyptian-Israeli Armistice Demarcation Line, with headquarters in Gaza. The complete withdrawal of Israeli forces took place on 8 March 1957.

The United Nations force continues its mission of safeguarding the peace along the demarcation line. A subsidiary organ of the United Nations Assembly, it consists of professional military units, of regulars under the command of career officers. They wear helmets or berets of United Nations blue colour, and have armbands with the United Nations emblem. Otherwise they are equipped with their national arms and uniforms.

The fact that UNEF came into existence was due to an exceptional combination of circumstances: the USSR and the United States were on the same side, and for at least three of the four States involved in the fighting, acceptance of the force was a way out of difficulties. A vital precedent for an international peace force was set, but there is still no chance of a permanent army to enforce United Nations decisions, unless the machinery provided in the Charter can be set in motion. UNEF is a purely provisional, emergency arrangement. As such it is an important factor in the maintenance of peace in a troubled area.

UNTSO keeps a watchful eye on the Israeli frontiers with Syria and Jordan, which are not screened by UNEF. There has not been, however, any progress towards a basic political solution and the Security Council continues to receive accusations and complaints, from both the Arab and the Israeli sides, of violation of the armistice agreements, of frontier attacks and acts of aggression. The complaints are dealt with by the established United Nations organs.

As for the Suez Canal, the United Nations undertook to clear it as soon as a cease-fire was declared. This task of clearance was completed in four months by an international salvage fleet, under the direction of the Secretary General. The International Bank for Reconstruction and Development was instrumental in bringing about an agreement providing for compensation between the holders of the Suez Canal Company shares and the Egyptian government. The United Kingdom and French governments concluded bilateral agreements with the United Arab Republic to liquidate mutual financial claims arising out of the conflict.

The Lebanese crisis. In the summer of 1958 the United Nations had to deal with yet another acute crisis which flared up in the Middle East. This time it was a conflict within the Arab group of States.

On 22 May 1958, Lebanon complained to the Security Council about the intervention of the United Arab Republic in its internal affairs, alleging infiltration of armed bands and arms from Syria, participation of United Arab Republic nationals in rebellion against the Government of Lebanon, the waging of a violent radio and press campaign calling for the overthrow of the Lebanese Government.

The Council decided to send a United Nations Observation Group urgently to Lebanon to watch the borders and to prevent infiltration of armed men and arms. Within a few days, direct and constant patrolling was made possible by some 150 military observers from 14 countries.

On 15 July United States armed forces landed in the Beirut area. The United States Government informed the Security Council that these forces landed at the request of the Government of Lebanon to help it 'to stabilize the situation brought on by the threats from outside, until such time as the United Nations can take necessary steps to protect the independence and political integrity of Lebanon'. The United States force would be withdrawn as soon as the United Nations could take over. Two days later, the United Kingdom announced that British paratroopers had started landing in Jordan in answer to an urgent appeal from King Hussein to help Jordan preserve its political independence and territorial integrity.

The Council held 11 meetings but no action could be taken, all the draft resolutions failing to obtain the required majority. Before the Council adjourned the Secretary General emphasized that the responsibility of the United Nations remained, and that the Observation Group in Lebanon would continue its work. 'The presence of the United Nations observers moving around in their white jeeps from village to village,' he said, 'was welcomed both by government supporters and by opposition elements.'

At an emergency special session on 21 August, the Assembly unanimously adopted a resolution sponsored by 10 Arab States, in which they pledged a good neighbour policy and co-operation for mutual benefit. The Secretary General was asked to make arrangements for facilitating the early withdrawal of foreign troops from Lebanon and Jordan.

In the meantime a new President was elected in Lebanon and appointed a new government which resumed normal relations with the United Arab Republic and asked the Council to delete the Lebanese question from the matters before it, stressing the important part played by the United Nations in bringing about harmony and co-operation between nations. The United States troops withdrew from Lebanon and the United Kingdom troops withdrew from Jordan, where a special representative of the Secretary General is watching the situation. The last United Nations observer left Beirut on 9 December 1958. At the peak of its activity the United Nations Observation Group had 591 military personnel of 21 countries, using 290 vehicles and manning 49 observation posts.

THE HUNGARIAN QUESTION

In the course of the eventful month of November 1956, not one but two emergency special sessions of the General Assembly were held; the second being convened to consider the critical situation in Hungary.

At the news of the outbreaks against the Hungarian Government followed by Soviet armed intervention to put down the rising, the Security Council met urgently on 28 October at the request of France, the United Kingdom and the United States. While accusations and counter-accusations were heard in the meetings of the Council, the Secretary General on 1 and 2 November received urgent appeals from the Hungarian Premier (Imre Nagy) requesting help to defend the country's neutrality and asking the Council to 'instruct the Soviet and

Hungarian governments to start immediately negotiations for the withdrawal of Soviet troops'. A resolution urging the USSR to end its intervention having been vetoed by the USSR, an emergency special Assembly was called, and on 4 November the USSR was again called on to cease intervention in Hungary.

Next day, the Secretary General received a cable from a new Hungarian Government under Janos Kadar stating that the appeals from the Nagy government to the United Nations had no legal value. The Assembly nevertheless continued to consider the question and once more asked the USSR to withdraw its forces and called for free elections to be held as soon as order was restored. The reaction of the Hungarian Government was negative. It refused a United Nations investigation of conditions in Hungary, but was ready to receive relief through the good offices of the United Nations. Later, at the regular session of the Assembly, the Hungarian delegation protested against keeping the Hungarian question on the agenda and declared it would not participate any further in the work of the session. The Assembly established a committee of five to investigate the situation in Hungary, but the Hungarian Government again refused all co-operation with the committee, which nevertheless prepared a comprehensive report based on testimony of witnesses heard in several countries, as well as on documentation from governmental and other sources.

Its main conclusions were that what had taken place in Hungary was a spontaneous national rising due to long-standing grievances. It had been entirely peaceful and the transformation of the demonstration into an armed uprising was due to the action of the secret police, the AVH, in opening fire on the people. The Nagy government had never issued an invitation to the Soviet troops to intervene. In the light of the extent of foreign intervention, consideration of the Hungarian question by the United Nations had been legally proper and moreover had been requested by a legal government of Hungary.

The Assembly, in 1957, noted the report, but its special representative, appointed to take steps to achieve United Nations objectives as regards Hungary, reported that his efforts were fruitless, the Hungarian and Soviet governments refusing any discussions or co-operation.

The Special Committee continued to watch the situation in Hungary. Following the announcement, in June 1958, that Imre Nagy, the prime minister during the rising, and three of his associates had been executed, it issued a report 'on the continued policy of repression' carried out in Hungary. The 1958 Assembly considered this report and denounced the executions. It decided to continue to watch the situation in Hungary, appointing Sir Leslie Munro, of New Zealand, a former President of the General Assembly, to watch the developments in Hungary and to report to the Assembly.

United Nations relief action in Hungary was more effective. The International Red Cross on behalf of the United Nations and with the co-operation of the Hungarian Red Cross organized the relief. A United Nations/Food and Agriculture Organization technical mission visited Budapest in January 1957 to inquire into needs for food, medicine and other supplies. Contributions from various sources amounted to $15 million enabling powdered milk and cod liver oil to be distributed to 173 thousand mothers and children, meals in schools to be given to 60 thousand children, relief packages to be delivered to some 150 thousand needy persons and medical supplies, blankets and coal to be sent to hospitals.

THE KOREAN QUESTION

United Nations action in defence of the Republic of Korea marked a significant step in the development of an organized, concerted collective international effort to safeguard the security of nations. The attack by North Korean forces on the Republic of Korea led to collective military assistance under United Nations auspices, given to the victim of aggression.

After the surrender of Japan in 1945, Korea had been occupied by the United States and the USSR with the 38th parallel as the dividing line. In August 1948 a government was established in the southern part which was henceforth known as the Republic of Korea. A separate government came into being in September in North Korea.

A seven-member Commission on Korea was set up by the 1948 Assembly to lend its good offices to attain the unification of all Korea. The commission reported no progress. It had observed the withdrawal of United States occupation forces from the south in June 1949, but not the reported withdrawal of those of the USSR in December 1948.

Invasion from the north. On 25 June 1950, the Secretary General was informed by the United Nations Commission on Korea and by the United States Government that North Korean forces had that morning invaded the Republic. The Security Council by a vote of 9 to 0, with the abstention of Yugoslavia and in the absence of the USSR declared that the armed attack was a breach of peace. (The USSR had withdrawn from the Council in January 1950, stating that it would not recognize as legal any decision of the Council until the representative of nationalist China, the 'Kuomintang' group, had been removed; the USSR returned to the Council in August 1950.)

The Council called for immediate cessation of hostilities and for the withdrawal of troops. The following day it asked United Nations members to furnish assistance to the Republic of Korea to repel the armed attack and to restore peace and security in the area. Fifty-one members expressed support for the stand taken by the Council. The USSR and four other members declared the Council's resolution to be illegal.

The United States announced that its sea, air and ground forces had been ordered to give support to the troops of the Republic of Korea. Sixteen more countries provided combatant units. Five nations supplied medical units. The Republic of Korea placed its military forces under the United Nations Unified Command.

Following the return of USSR to the Security Council and the use by it of the negative vote, the Council failed henceforth to reach any substantive decision in the Korean question, which was aggravated by the intervention of the forces of the People's Republic of China in support of North Korea. The Assembly took over the question and directed its efforts towards the cessation of hostilities.

The armistice. In Korea itself the fighting front was stabilized in the spring of 1951 near the 38th parallel. After prolonged negotiations, an armistice agreement was signed on 27 July 1953, and hostilities ceased. A demarcation line and a demilitarized zone were established and United Nations machinery was created to supervise the carrying-out of the agreement.

The political conference, suggested in the armistice agreement, was convened in Geneva in July 1954, but failed to reach an agreed solution on the reunification of Korea. No progress has been made since, but the agreement remains in force. Subsequent Assemblies have reaffirmed United Nations objectives in Korea—the establishment by peaceful means of a unified, independent and democratic Korea—but the country remains divided.

Parallel to political action in Korea, the United Nations has undertaken the task of rehabilitating the war-devastated country. As soon as the hostilities had come to an end, the United Nations Korean Reconstruction Agency undertook large-scale reconstruction and economic aid. Food, livestock and raw materials were imported to meet the most urgent needs. The irrigation system for rice cultivation was restored and extended; the fishing fleet was reconstructed; equipment was supplied to textile mills; cement plants were modernized and new ones constructed; output of coal-mines was increased through introduction of modern machinery. Material was made available for the construction or repair of thousands of class-rooms; new textbook printing plants have been built, vocational centres created.

Particular attention was paid to housing and construction of low cost homes and to medical and welfare services. The total cost of the United Nations relief for Korea amounted to $480 million contributed by

39 countries, of which $444 million came from governments and the rest from non-governmental organizations, Specialized Agencies, etc.

KASHMIR

On the creation of independent India and Pakistan in 1947, the princedom of Jammu and Kashmir was free to accede to either State. On 1 January 1948, India reported to the Security Council that tribesmen and other armed groups had invaded the state of Jammu and Kashmir and extensive fighting was taking place. The Maharajah of the state subsequently requested accession to India, which agreed on the understanding that once normal conditions were restored, the question of accession 'should be settled by a reference to the people'. India also contended that Pakistan was assisting the invasion. Pakistan denied it, and declared that the accession to India was illegal.

The Council set up a commission of three for investigation and mediation. After an inquiry on the spot, the commission proposed to India and to Pakistan a cease-fire and a truce agreement. Cease-fire was ordered as from 1 January 1949 and United Nations observers were appointed to report on the execution of the cease-fire on an agreed line.

Later the Council named a United Nations representative for India and Pakistan to bring about demilitarization of the area and to prepare the holding of a plebiscite. The representative negotiated a number of proposals with the governments of India and Pakistan—but without tangible results. In May 1958, there were recommendations for a renewed pledge by the two governments to create an atmosphere favourable to future negotiations, for a reaffirmation of the integrity of the cease-fire line, and for the calling of a Prime Ministers' conference between India and Pakistan. India declared itself unable to agree to these recommendations.

ALGERIA

Soon after the outbreak of the rebellion in Algeria, in November 1954, Saudi Arabia brought to the attention of the Security Council the 'grave situation in Algeria'. In July 1955 the Asian and African group of States asked that the question of Algeria be included in the agenda of the tenth session of the Assembly. France opposed this on the ground that Algerian affairs were essentially within the French Government's domestic juridiction. The French delegation withdrew from the Assembly in protest against a debate which they regarded as being in defiance of the provisions of the Charter. A procedural motion not to consider the question was finally adopted, but the Algerian problem has been on the agenda of all subsequent Assemblies despite repeated French objections.

In 1958 a resolution which would have had the Assembly recognize the right of the Algerian people to independence and which urged negotiations between France and Algeria, failed to receive the required two-thirds majority.

Similarly, in 1959, the plenary session of the Assembly failed to adopt a resolution of the Political Committee which 'noting with satisfaction that the two parties concerned have accepted the right of self-determination as the basis for the solution of the Algerian problem', urged the two parties to determine the conditions necessary to implement as early as possible the right of self-determination of the Algerian people, including conditions for a cease-fire.

RACE CONFLICTS IN SOUTH AFRICA

At each of its thirteen sessions, except the fourth, the Assembly has carried on its agenda the item 'treatment of people of Indian origin in the Union of South Africa'. This item arises out of the complaint of the Indian Government that the Union enacted discriminatory legislation against Indians, segregating them commercially and residentially, in violation of an agreement between the two countries defining the status of South African Indians. The Assembly repeatedly stated that this impaired friendly relations between the two countries and appealed to the Union to respect its obligations. The Union refused to accept consecutive recommendations of the Assembly on a matter which it considered to be within its domestic jurisdiction.

In 1952, a related, and more general, problem of race discrimination in South Africa, that of 'apartheid' (segregation), was brought before the Assembly which, stressing the principle of racial equality and condemning race discrimination, established a three-man commission to study the racial situation in the Union. South Africa declared that the resolutions violated the provisions of the Charter precluding intervention in matters of domestic jurisdiction.

The commission, basing its report on a study of legislation and of documents, on statements of witnesses, etc.—owing to the refusal of South Africa to co-operate—presented several reports to the Assembly, stating that the doctrine of racial superiority on which the policy of apartheid is based was scientifically false, dangerous to peace and international relations and contrary to the 'dignity and worth of the human person'. An eighth consecutive resolution on the subject was voted by the Assembly in 1959 expressing regret and concern that the Union had not responded to the appeals of the Assembly for equal rights and fundamental freedoms of all racial groups. The South African delegation has refused to sit in the committee of the Assembly while the item is discussed.

Course IV

ECONOMIC AND SOCIAL PROBLEMS
APPLICATION OF ARTICLE 55
OF THE CHARTER

Responsibility for United Nations functions in carrying out the principle of the Preamble 'to promote social progress and better standards of life in larger freedom' (as set forth in detail in Article 55 of the Charter) has been vested in the Economic and Social Council (Ecosoc) which, in the view of many students of the United Nations, is potentially the most important organ in the world body.

ECOSOC CONSTITUTION AND WORKING METHODS

All 18 members of Ecosoc are elected for a term of three years. The renewal of the Council takes place every year through the election of six members. Retiring members are eligible for re-election. Each member has one vote, all decisions being taken by simple majority. The Council may invite to its meetings, without voting rights and whenever it considers fit, any member of the United Nations and any of the Specialized Agencies; and it makes its own arrangements for consultation with the non-governmental organizations. Any Member State may be represented at the meetings of Ecosoc by an observer, who may make statements but has no voting rights.

Ecosoc normally holds two sessions each year, one in the spring in New York, the other in the summer in Geneva. The summer session is resumed during the General Assembly.

The technical and specialized work of this central policy-making and co-ordinating organ of the United Nations for economic and social questions is done by a number of subsidiary bodies—in the first place by its functional commissions: on Human Rights, on the Status of Women, the Social Commission, on Narcotic Drugs, on International Commodity Trade (each of 18 members) and by the Statistical and Population Commissions (each of 15 members).

There are four regional economic commissions: for Europe, for Asia and the Far East, for Latin America and for Africa.

Other bodies related to Ecosoc are: the Permanent Opium Board and the Drug Supervisory Body, the United Nations Children's Fund, the Technical Assistance Board, the Administrative Committee on Co-ordination (the Secretary General of the United Nations and the executive heads of the Specialized Agencies).

A most important function of Ecosoc is that of relationship with the Specialized Agencies which have international responsibilities in economic, social, cultural, educational, health and related fields, and consideration of their activities.

ECONOMIC QUESTIONS

Early in its life, in 1947, the Council was asked by the Assembly to review each year the economic situation of the world. Background for this debate is provided by the annual *World Economic Report* and by special reports on particular problems or regions. By now these studies form a unique and imposing library on the state of present-day world economy and its problems.

The debates in the Council on the international economic situation have led to decisions by the Council and the Assembly; they have formed the basis of United Nations work in the field of economic development, and, in particular, of concerted action for the development of those parts of the world which are economically underdeveloped.

One of the most frequently recurring problems of world economy is that of stability in relation to economic expansion, and especially of inflationary pressures caused by a high level of economic activity and the processes of development, as well as the question of maintaining full and productive employment.

Expansion of world trade is another problem closely followed by Ecosoc; it deals with the removal of obstacles to international exchange, such as barriers imposed for reasons of balance of payments; with the development of inter-regional trade, in particular East-West trade; and with the situation of countries which depend on exports of relatively few commodities.

In the related field of international commodity problems, the Council examines measures to avoid excessive fluctuations in the prices of primary commodities, and it keeps under review the situation of world commodity markets. This is of the utmost importance for the underdeveloped countries, most of them being producers of raw materials, and suffering from violent and sudden falls and rises of prices over which they have no control.

Agreements have been concluded under the auspices of the United

Nations in respect of a number of primary commodities. In March 1959 a new Wheat Agreement was concluded for three years to promote the expansion of free trade in wheat, overcoming the effects of burdensome surpluses and critical shortages, and to encourage the consumption of wheat. A United Nations Sugar Conference in 1958, with an agreement of five years' duration revised the mechanism of quotas and the fixing of prices. An agreement on tin fixed the prices of that important commodity. Studies on rubber, cotton, wool, tea and olive oil are in progress.

In the debates on commodities, attention has been given to the possibility of establishing a world food reserve. The Food and Agriculture Organization is studying ways and means of establishing stocks of food, national and international, which would be promptly available in case of need.

THE UNDERDEVELOPED AREAS

During one of the speeches on the occasion of the tenth anniversary of Ecosoc in 1956, it was said that the Council's most important achievement had been to create world consciousness of the problem of underdevelopment and the widening gap between the industrialized countries and the underdeveloped areas. From this awareness of the need to help economic development emerged the programmes of technical assistance and the plans for financing economic development. Many of the problems on the agenda of Ecosoc—such as measures for increasing productivity, industrialization, balanced economic growth, land reform, conservation and utilization of resources and energy—are mainly problems of the less fortunate parts of the world.

The most important problem is that of financing economic development and of promoting an accelerated flow of both public and private capital to underdeveloped areas. The International Finance Corporation was set up to provide capital for productive private ventures, but it cannot meet the need for financing the basic economic infra-structure— facilities such as roads, power stations, schools, hospitals and government buildings—nor can the International Bank.

As a result of numerous studies it was proposed to create a Special United Nations Fund for Economic Development (SUNFED) to finance what is described as 'non-self-liquidating projects' on a grant-in-aid basis. The lack of progress in establishing the Fund was caused by the fact that many governments, including some of the most important potential contributors, link the financing of economic development with disarmament and savings on defence expenditure, i.e., with global political solutions.

In the meantime, however, the Assembly in 1958 decided to create a

Special Fund as an extension of the existing technical assistance activities.[1]

On specialized questions of economic development numerous studies were made on rapid industrialization of underdeveloped countries, stressing the need for co-ordinating industrial diversification with the development of agricultural production and for co-operation to facilitate better use of manpower, natural resources and productive equipment.

Considerable attention is paid to the role of agrarian reform in economic progress. Technical advice and assistance are available from the United Nations and the Specialized Agencies for implementing land reform measures, the organization of co-operatives and low cost housing construction.

A United Nations Scientific Conference on Conversation and Utilization of Resources held in 1949 resulted in decisions by Ecosoc on international action for conserving and utilizing non-agricultural wealth, such as iron ore, non-ferrous metals and energy resources, on which an interesting study was prepared: 'New sources of energy and economic development—solar energy, wind energy, tidal energy, geothermic energy and thermal energy of the seas.'

In surveying the world's resources particular attention was paid to water and the necessity to husband available supplies. The demand for water for domestic, agricultural, industrial and energy use is growing steadily, and a shortage of water supplies is already slowing down economic development in many areas. In accordance with a 1958 decision of Ecosoc, a Water Resources Development Centre was established in 1959 at United Nations Headquarters to co-ordinate efforts for the development of water resources. United Nations organs also co-operate with the Advisory Committee on Arid Zone Research set up by Unesco.

Much practical work has been done to facilitate transport, communications and tourism through international agreements on road traffic, on road signals and signs, and other conventions. The Council asked governments to encourage tourism by improving transport and hotel services and by simplifying visa and frontier formalities and customs inspections.

The United Nations publishes three basic reference works: the *Statistical Yearbook*, a comprehensive world-wide collection of data; the *Demographic Yearbook*, statistics of world population; and the monthly *Bulletin of Statistics*, which contains current data on more than sixty subjects from 140 countries and territories.

In the field of international tax relations the Council urged governments to conclude bilateral agreements to avoid double taxation and

---

1. For details see the chapter on technical assistance, page 76.

advocated stimulation of the flow of capital to underdeveloped countries through tax incentives.

REGIONAL ECONOMIC COMMISSIONS

To facilitate concerted action aimed at raising the level of economic activity in their respective regions and to maintain and strengthen economic relations between the countries of a region and with other parts of the world, four regional economic commissions have been established by the United Nations—for Europe (ECE), for Asia and the Far East (ECAFE), for Latin America (ECLA), and for Africa (ECA).

In the course of more than ten years' existence the first three commissions have become a most effective instrument of international economic action within the framework of the United Nations system. Each plays a vital role in the economic development and integration of its region and contributes to the growth of trade and industrial co-operation between regions. Organized on a common pattern, the commissions adapted their working methods and their technical activities to the needs and conditions of their regions, and therein lies much of their strength and usefulness.

Economic Commission for Europe (ECE)

ECE, the first regional commission, was set up in March 1947, with its headquarters in Geneva, at the Palais des Nations. It is virtually an all-European body, its members being all the 29 European countries and the United States. Representatives of the German Democratic Republic participate in the work of the technical committees of ECE.

In its early days, ECE had to deal with emergency problems arising out of the economic dislocation caused by the war: allocation of scarce material, such as coal, metallurgical coke, pit-props for coal-mines.

Most of the work of the commission is carried out on a technical level and is done in committees and working parties. These meet in private throughout the year for business discussions between experts from all over Europe. The following is a brief catalogue of some of the work done by the technical bodies of ECE:

Energy: facilitating the exchange and transfer of electric current across national frontiers; promoting agricultural electrification, production, utilization and distribution of sources of energy such as coal, natural gas and oil; production of power from nuclear reactors.

Transport: simplifying custom formalities for goods and for tourists; plans for a unified European main road system; standardization of railway stock, rates, costs, moving of perishable goods.

Housing: studies of costs, of house-building and production methods; technical problems such as mechanization and prefabrication; study trips to various countries.

Agriculture: promotion of trade in agricultural products between various European regions; standardization and quality control of perishable foodstuffs, such as vegetables, fish and fruit.

Development of trade: promotion of trade within Europe and with other regions; extension of East-West exchanges; payment compensation operations; co-ordination of fairs and exhibitions.

A *Survey of European Economy* is issued early in the year for the annual session of ECE. A quarterly *Economic Bulletin for Europe* is published, as well as statistical bulletins on coal, timber, steel, housing, energy and transport.

The secretariat of ECE is headed by Mr. Sakari Tuomioja, of Finland.

Economic Commission for Asia and the Far East (ECAFE)

This Commission's work methods are determined by the degree of economic development in its region and the problems it faces. ECAFE differs from ECE in so far as it covers a much wider geographical area and most of the countries in the region fall into the category of 'under-developed'.

The region includes: Afghanistan, Burma, Cambodia, Ceylon, China, India, Indonesia, Iran, Japan, Korea, Laos, Malaya, Nepal, Pakistan, the Philippines, Thailand and Viet-Nam (all members of the commission), Brunei, Hong Kong, British Borneo and Sarawak and Singapore (associate members without voting rights). Other countries outside the area, but with interest in it are full members of ECAFE. Among these are: Australia, France, the Netherlands, New Zealand, the USSR, the United Kingdom and the United States.

ECAFE was established in March 1947: its headquarters are in Bangkok, at Sala Santihan (Peace Hall), Thailand.

The first task of the commission was to carry out a survey of the basic problems of economic development and studies of techniques of programming economic action suitable to the region. This was followed by recommendations to governments, the majority of which have been accepted and put into effect.

Industrialization is one of the main problems facing ECAFE, with the purpose of raising the standard of living, finding employment for the rapidly growing populations and meeting the demands for consumption goods produced domestically. Particular attention is paid to training of personnel for industrial development, especially in the iron and steel industry.

A most urgent problem in the area is the supply of electric power.

The commission keeps abreast of progress in the use of atomic energy for industrial purposes, to meet the keen interest of the Asian countries with scarce supplies of coal and other sources of energy.

The work on housing and building material resulted in the creation of a regional research centre in Indonesia for dealing with problems of building in humid climates and of one in India for research into such problems in hot dry climates.

Technical studies and advisory services assist the region in combatting its transport deficiencies, in building low cost roads and in modernizing railways. For inland navigation which is of great importance in the area, a convention was drafted for uniform systems of vessel measurements to facilitate international traffic.

A Bureau of Flood Control and Water Resources Development, a section of the secretariat of ECAFE, works out on a regional scale measures for controlling floods, the scourge of Asia. Work is in progress on a development plan for the water resources in the Lower Mekong River basin, an area of approximately 235 thousand miles. Irrigation alone would provide some 23 million acres of new arable land.

The commission's annual *Economic Survey of Asia and the Far East* serves not only as a source of information and reference, but also to formulate policies.

U Nyun of Burma is the Executive Secretary of ECAFE.

Economic Commission for Latin America (ECLA)

The third regional economic commission was founded in February 1948 with headquarters in Santiago, Chile. It differs from the other commissions in organization and methods of work, since its region is linguistically and culturally more uniform, and since there is less variation in the level of economic development of its members.

All the American republics south of United States are members of the commission, together with France, the Netherlands, the United Kingdom and the United States.

Economic development and industrialization are naturally the main objectives of ECLA. The commission assists the governments in programming their industrial development and in training technical personnel. A meeting of experts of the iron and steel industry in Bogotá, and later in São Paulo, brought together more than 200 technicians from the region and other parts to discuss the development of natural resources and the creation of domestic steel industries. A similar conference was held in Buenos Aires on pulp and paper problems.

Assistance is given to improve the agrarian structure of Latin American countries, and to solve the problem of relative underdevelopment of agriculture and livestock breeding in many parts of the region.

A Trade Commitee works in the direction of a multilateral payment system, the extension of certain industries on the basis of a multilateral regional market, and generally the development of trade within the region.

Integration of the economies of the Central American republics of Costa Rica, El Salvador, Guatemala, Honduras, and Nicaragua is one of the tasks handled by ECLA.

The Executive Secretary of the commission is Dr. Raúl Prebitsch, of Argentina.

Economic Commission for Africa (ECA)

The terms of reference of this youngest of the four commissions are similar to those of the other three, with emphasis laid, however, on raising the level of economic activity and standards of living and on maintaining and strengthening the economic relations of African countries and territories both among themselves and with other parts of the world.

ECA held its first meeting in January 1959 in the capital of Ethiopia, Addis Ababa, which is the headquarters of the commission.

There were four independent African States, which became members of the United Nations in 1945. Ten independent African countries were represented at the first ECA session: Ethiopia, Ghana, Guinea, Liberia, Libya, Morocco, Sudan, Tunisia, United Arab Republic and the Union of South Africa. Belgium, France, Italy, Portugal and the United Kingdom are also members of the commission. Other African States are approaching full nationhood and can soon be expected to join the United Nations and become members of ECA.

In the course of the first session the Executive Secretary of ECA described the task of the commission as being nothing less than the transformation of the social life of African peoples from low subsistence living and tribal organization to modern rural and urbanized societies. It needs good planning, preceded by extensive research and study and also international aid, to help new African States to base their independence on a viable economy.

Throughout the debates of the commission stress was laid on the need for United Nations assistance to the newly independent countries of Africa and the necessity of co-operation between neighbouring African countries. The first task of the Commission should be that of promoting the economic independence of the continent.

The programme of work, as decided in the course of the session, calls for a study of increased contacts between West African countries and territories, in the sphere of water conservation, international use of roads, railways and harbours, pooling of electric power and control of fisheries. A study is also to be made on different aspects of a Maghreb economic unit.

In co-operation with the Food and Agriculture Organization, effective locust control will be studied on an all-African basis, as well as the eradication of infectious livestock diseases.

A long-term statistical survey is to be undertaken on the conservation of natural resources of the continent and on capital formation.

Mr. Mekki Abbas, Sudan, is the Executive Secretary of ECA.

BIBLIOGRAPHICAL REFERENCE

ASHER, R. E. *The United Nations and economic and social co-operation.* Washington, Brookings Institution, 1957. 561 p.

Course V

HUMANITARIAN AND SOCIAL WORK

PART I

HUMAN RIGHTS

'To reaffirm faith in fundamental human rights, in the dignity and worth of the human person, in the equal rights of men and women and of nations large and small'—this is one of the principal aims of the United Nations, as set forth in the Preamble to the Charter. Human rights are referred to in six different articles of the Charter, and Article 68 specifically prescribes the creation of a commission 'for the promotion of human rights'.

This Commission on Human Rights, with 18 members, declared at its first session, in January 1947, that its immediate aim was to draft an international bill of rights, conceived in three parts: a Declaration, a Covenant, and Measures of Implementation.

The Declaration was proclaimed by the General Assembly in Paris on 10 December 1948. Of the then 58 Member States, 48 voted for, 0 against, 8 abstained and 2 were absent during the vote.

UNIVERSAL DECLARATION OF HUMAN RIGHTS

The 30 articles of the Declaration set forth man's inalienable rights in the civic, political, economic, social and cultural fields; the right to life, liberty and security of the person; to freedom from arbitrary arrest; to a fair trial; to privacy; to freedom of movement and residence; to social security, work and education; to nationality; to freedom of worship, of expression, of peaceful assembly; to take part in the government of his country, to hold public office, to seek and be granted asylum and to own property. The Assembly proclaimed these rights as 'a common standard of achievement for all peoples and all nations', and called upon all Member States to give the widest publicity and dissemination to the

Declaration, principally in schools and other educational institutions.

The Declaration has been translated and distributed in some fifty languages. In 1950, the date of 10 December was proclaimed by the Assembly as Human Rights Day, to be observed each year. Unesco has assumed a special role in spreading a better understanding of human rights and disseminating the Declaration. Pamphlets, radio scripts, films and filmstrips, posters and exhibition material on the subject are distributed in large quantities throughout the world.

The Declaration has no binding legal value, but it has great political and moral authority and has had a definite impact on the thinking and practice of the United Nations itself and of governments, when dealing with problems relating to human rights. It has been invoked in the United Nations almost as frequently as the Charter itself. It is reflected in many international treaties; its influence is apparent in national constitutions; it has been quoted in legal decisions. Guarantees of human rights were given in the 1947 peace treaties with Bulgaria, Hungary, Finland, Italy and Rumania, by Japan in 1951 and in the State Treaty of 1955 by Austria.

SLOW PROGRESS OF THE COVENANT

Yet progress has been slow since 1948 in drafting the Covenant of Human Rights and the Measures of Implementation, the two other parts of the Bill of Rights. By 1958 the Assembly got as far as giving consideration to a few substantive articles of the draft on economic, social and cultural rights.

The drafts of the covenants—one to cover political and civil rights, and the other to deal with economic, social and cultural rights—have an identical preamble, with much of the language taken from the Declaration—recognizing the 'inherent dignity and . . . equal and inalienable rights' of man. Also common is Article I, on the right to self-determination.

The draft on economic and social rights contains obligations by States concerning the realization of these rights; it lists the right to work, to just and favourable conditions of work, to trade unions, to social security, rights relating to the family, motherhood and childhood, to an adequate standard of living and to care of health; to education, to science and culture. It provides for a reporting system as the only international measure of implementation.

In the draft on civil and political rights each State undertakes to respect and to ensure to all individuals within its territory the rights of the covenant and to give effect to these rights. These are: the right to life, the prohibition of inhuman and degrading treatment, prohibition of slavery and forced labour, the right to liberty and security of the person, liberty of movement, the right to a fair trial and equality before the law, freedom of thought, conscience, religion, opinion, expression and assembly and the right of association.

A Human Rights Committee, elected by the International Court of Justice, would hear and mediate disputes between States over alleged violation of the rights in the covenant. States would have to report on the steps taken to give effect to the covenant.

Each year, the United Nations receives several thousand communications concerning human rights from individuals and groups in all parts of the world. As the United Nations is an intergovernmental organization it does not as a rule deal with complaints from private individuals or groups about violations of human rights. The Secretariat forwards copies of the communications to the governments concerned without, however, disclosing the identity of the authors except with their consent. Whether any government takes any action on any communication thus forwarded is entirely at its own discretion. The Secretariat also prepares confidential lists of the communications for the information of the Commission on Human Rights and the Commission on the Status of Women.

The 1958 Assembly again considered the draft covenants, but their examination was postponed until the 1959 session. In the meantime the Human Rights Commission at its 1959 session unanimously adopted a draft Declaration of the Rights of the Child. The dratf was submitted to the General Assembly which, after making some amendments, also unanimously adopted the Declaration and urged the widest dissemination for it.

While uncertainty persists as to how long it will take to complete the covenants, important decisions were taken by Ecosoc in 1956 to undertake certain activities until such time as the covenants come in force. Member States were requested to report every three years on the progress achieved in the field of human rights and on measures taken to safeguard human liberty in their countries. The Assembly has also established a programme of advisory services in the field of human rights, entailing the sending out of experts, and provision of fellowships and seminars.

Prevention of discrimination and protection of minorities is dealt with by a special sub-commission of the Human Rights Commission. Governments are being consulted on the desirability of preparing an international instrument setting forth the principles of how to eradicate discrimination in education and Unesco had been asked to draft such an instrument. The sub-commission has also been discussing discriminatory practices in employment and occupation, and has entrusted to the International Labour Organisation (ILO) the task of surveying them. Reports are prepared on religious rights and practices and on political rights. ILO adopted in June 1958 a convention and recommendation calling for steps to be taken to eliminate discrimination in respect of employment and occupation on the basis of race, colour, sex, religion, political opinion, national extraction or social origin.

In co-operation with ILO, Ecosoc established an international procedure for safeguarding trade union rights, to receive and to consider complaints from governments, trade unions or employers' associations which allege infringement of trade union rights. Also in co-operation with ILO, the United Nations has been engaged in studying the problem of forced labour and the means to be used in abolishing it. This resulted in the adoption by ILO in 1957 of a draft Convention on Forced Labour.

A supplementary Convention on the Abolition of Slavery was adopted at a conference in Geneva in 1956. This asks for the abolition of debt bondage, serfdom and bride-price, and it provides measures for suppressing the slave trade (which still persists in certain areas), and for international co-operation in implementing the convention.

A draft of a declaration on the right of asylum has been circulated to governments for comment. This draft states that every person whose life, physical integrity or liberty is threatened in violation of the principles of the Human Rights Declaration should be entitled to asylum and not expelled, returned or rejected.

A legacy of the war, the question of prisoners of war not repatriated or accounted for, was dealt with by an *ad hoc* commission of the United Nations. Its good offices led to the repatriation of some 29,000 Germans from the USSR and 34,000 Japanese from China, war prisoners and detained civilians, and a small number of Italians, Austrians and Spaniards.

Another war legacy, the disappearance, without any evidence of death, of millions of human beings, resulting from deportation and extermination by the Nazis, had given rise to many legal difficulties as regards heritage, remarriage, etc. A United Nations convention established an International Bureau for the Declaration of Death in Geneva, which issues lists of declarations of death. These are accepted as legal evidence of death.

A Yearbook of Human Rights has been published regularly since 1946. Starting with a compilation of declarations and bills of rights in force in various countries as of 31 December 1946, it published constitutional provisions and legislative texts on human rights, together with provisions on these rights in international treaties and surveys of United Nations activities in this field.

STATUS OF WOMEN

Equal rights of men and women are singled out in that sentence of the preamble to the Charter which reaffirms 'faith in fundamental human rights'. A Commission on the Status of Women is working on problems of political equality, equality before the law, the right to education and economic opportunities of women.

A Convention on the Political Rights of Women was adopted by the General Assembly in 1952. As of June 1960 it has been ratified by 34 States. Parties to this convention agree to give women the right to vote, to be elected to office, to hold public office and perform public functions, on equal terms with men.

In 1956 the Assembly voted a Convention on the Nationality of Married Women. Under this convention a celebration of a dissolution of marriage between a national of a contracting State and an alien should not have automatic effect on the wife's nationality. Acquisition of the husband's nationality is made voluntary.

In the field of family laws and women's property rights, the commission recommended equality of parental laws and duties, the right of a married woman to have a legal domicile independently of the husband, the right to work without the husband's authorization, equal rights to family property during marriage, and equitable sharing of property on dissolution. Particular attention is paid to the question of child marriage in some regions of the world, and to the fact that the free consent of both parties was not universally required as a condition for the validity of marriage. The deliberations and the resolutions of the Commission in these matters have a marked effect on the legislation and the customs of the countries involved.

ILO regularly reports to the commission on the situation concerning equal pay for equal work for women, and equality as regards working conditions and social insurance.

The commission has also urged that there should be no sex discrimination as regards access to all levels of education; that there should be equitable distribution of scholarships and access to training for all careers.

Co-operation with the non-governmental organizations is closer in the field of women's rights than in many others. This is particularly the case with women's organizations, which serve as a most effective vehicle for spreading knowledge about what the United Nations has done to secure equal rights for men and women.

FREEDOM OF INFORMATION

Two years before the proclamation of the Universal Declaration of Human Rights, the General Assembly announced that 'freedom of information is a fundamental human right, and the touchstone of all the freedoms to which the United Nations is consecrated'. This has since been the basis for a wide study of various aspects of freedom of information, of the rights, obligations and practices involved, and of professional and technical problems connected with the free flow of information across frontiers.

A United Nations conference on freedom of information was called in Geneva in 1948 and attended by 54 governments. It prepared three draft conventions, and adopted a large number of resolutions on various aspects of freedom of information.

The draft of a General Convention on Freedom of Information contains provisions to secure freedom to seek, to receive, and to impart information and opinions through any media, without government interference and regardless of frontiers. It prohibits discriminatory regulations or control of means of communication for information purposes. These guarantees would be subject to permissible clearly defined restrictions.

The draft on the International Right of Correction gives a State the right to demand a correction of what it considers to be false or distorted news capable of injuring its relations with other States, or its national dignity. In the case of refusal to publish a correction, a State may ask the Secretary General to circulate the correction through his information channels.

The third draft was that of a Convention on the Gathering and International Transmission of News. This obliges contracting parties to facilitate the entry, residence and travel of foreign correspondents, to secure them treatment on an equal basis, together with equal access to sources of news and to transmission facilities, and it also requires the contracting parties not to impose censorship or to cause delays in transmission in peace-time.

Of these drafts only the International Right of Correction has been approved and opened for signature by the Assembly. This was done in 1952; it has not yet come into force. The articles of the draft Convention on International Transmission of News have been approved by the Assembly, but have not been opened for signature.

The General Convention has been under discussion by the Assembly and other organs of the United Nations for several years but has not yet reached the stage of completion. A final text was drafted for consideration by the 1960 General Assembly.

In the meantime certain other aspects of the problem have come under review by the United Nations and the Specialized Agencies.

A Sub-commission on Freedom of Information which met from 1947 to 1952, drafted an International Code of Ethics. It suggested calling an international professional conference to prepare the final text of a code of ethics for the information profession, but the Assembly decided against this, asking merely for the draft text to be transmitted to information agencies 'for such use as they deem proper'.

At its fourteenth session, in 1952, Ecosoc appointed Salvador P. Lopez (Philippines) to prepare a report on contemporary problems and developments in the field of freedom of information. The Lopez report, submitted to the seventeenth session, in 1953, covered political and technical problems affecting freedom of information, and contained recommendations for action by the United Nations and interested Specialized Agencies, including Unesco, the International Telecommunication Union (ITU) and the Food and Agriculture Organization (FAO).

In 1955 the Secretary General prepared reports for Ecosoc on a programme to promote among news personnel a wider knowledge of the United Nations, of foreign countries, and of international affairs; as well as on current practices of censoring outgoing news dispatches; on the protection of sources of information of news personnel; on legal aspects of the rights and responsibilities of media of information; and on public and private monopolies and their effect on freedom of information. Unesco and ITU prepared a study on the transmission problems of press messages. The Council examined these reports in May 1955, and urged all States to cease peace-time censorship of outgoing news dispatches and to facilitate the unhindered transmission of news.

Previously the Assembly had urged Member States to grant correspondents who are accredited to the United Nations and the Specialized Agencies free access to countries where United Nations meetings are held and to all public information sources and services of the United Nations; to refrain from interfering with radio signals and from broadcasting unfair attacks against other peoples; to implement administrative measures suggested in two studies on the status and the work of foreign correspondents; and to offer facilities to foreign correspondents and students of journalism, including the granting of visas and currency.

In 1958 the Assembly asked Ecosoc to formulate a programme of concrete action, with measures to be taken at the international level for developing information enterprises in underdeveloped countries and for building adequate information media.

Meanwhile Ecosoc in the summer of 1959 approved and transmitted to the General Assembly a draft Declaration on Freedom of Information which sets out the right of everybody to information and to expression; the obligation on governments to protect the free flow of information; the principle that the press and other information media should serve the people and that all media should inform honestly and in good faith.

Thus in the course of 12 years of work on freedom of information the United Nations has considered three draft conventions, of which one has been opened for signature; it has adopted a number of recommendations and requests to governments, which are to a large extent substitutes for the conventions and are not binding; and it has examined many most valuable reports and studies.

The co-operation of the Specialized Agencies—of FAO, ILO, ITU, Unesco and the Universal Postal Union (UPU)—has been of great value to the United Nations in its work on freedom of information. Unesco, in particular, has assisted in all stages of the work, mainly in the preparation of studies on the development of information media and on technical questions. FAO helped in studying newsprint problems; ILO, the problem of the economic independence of news personnel; and ITU and UPU have helped in dealing with questions of transmission. Professional organizations of journalists and the information enterprises have been regularly consulted.

SOCIAL POLICIES AND SOCIAL SERVICES

A social welfare programme and practical assistance to governments form an important part of the economic and social development work of the United Nations. The main purpose is to assist the governments of underdeveloped countries to raise the standard of living of their peoples by improving social conditions.

Particular attention is paid to the growth of populations in the world and to the resulting urgent need of increasing production of food and goods; to the problem of housing and the need for adequate social services in order to avoid misery and increased delinquency among the new urban populations and the inhabitants of rural districts who have moved to cities in search of employment and amenities; and to the interdependence of social progress and industrial development.

The United Nations assists national governments in formulating and carrying out their national policies and programmes in housing construction and planning; in financing building for lower income groups; and in studying physical planning as an integral part of development plans.

In view of the particularly rapid growth of the populations of Asia, Africa, and Latin America, in the underdeveloped areas of the world, and because of the problems thus raised, population studies by the United Nations are focused on the population trends in these regions and their implications for economic and social policies and action. Regional centres for demographic training and research have been created under technical assistance.

In handling the related problem of migration and its demographic and social aspects, international action is concentrated (a) on promoting migratory movements beneficial to the development of both emigration and immigration countries; (b) on assuring adequate standards of living for migrants and equal treatment; (c) on social and cultural integration.

Close co-operation is maintained with non-governmental organizations active in providing services to emigrants.

Practical assistance is given to governments within the framework of social welfare activities. Out of the emergency action to meet the needs of children and families after the war grew the permanent programme of family, child and youth welfare in co-operation with the United Nations Children's Fund, involving care of the aged and rehabilitation of the handicapped. Governments are assisted in their social welfare work through social service advisers and experts, fellowships and seminars, and by means of documentation.

In the field of social defence, effective international co-operation on problems of crime and punishment has been organized and standard minimum rules established for the treatment of prisoners. In 1949 the Assembly adopted a Convention for the Suppression of the Traffic in Persons and the Exploitation of the Prostitution of Others.

A Convention on the Recovery of Maintenance Abroad (1956) is intended to afford a means of overcoming legal and practical difficulties faced by dependents (mainly women and children) who are seeking to obtain support from persons responsible for their maintenance but situated in another country.

PART II

UNITED NATIONS CHILDREN'S FUND (UNICEF)

In the world-wide battle against disease, under-nourishment and poor living conditions, Unicef leads the campaign for the welfare and health of the child and the mother. It was established as a temporary post-war emergency organ by the 1946 Assembly, to assist needy children in war-devastated areas. Since completion of the emergency work during the first post-war years in Europe and in the Far East, Unicef has been gradually evolving into an institution conducting a permanent campaign.

The Assembly confirmed the changed character of the fund by requesting it in 1950 to meet 'through the provision of supplies, training and advice, the emergency and longer range needs of children, with a view to strengthening the permanent child health and child welfare programmes of the countries receiving assistance', particularly in under-developed areas.

A permanent organ of the United Nations

In 1953 the Assembly decided that the Fund should continue indefinitely. It dropped 'emergency' from its name, but retained the title Unicef.

The Fund is financed by voluntary contributions from governments and individuals, not through the regular United Nations budget. A sum of $24 million was allocated to its various projects in 1959. It is estimated that the sum of $28 million will be needed for projects in 1960. Another source of revenue is the annual sale of greeting cards, which are designed by well-known artists from many countries. A profit of more than $750,000 was made from the 1959 sale of cards, over 14 million cards having been sold.

More than 55 million children and nursing and pregnant mothers benefited in 1959 from Unicef-aided programmes in more than 100 countries and territories. Three-quarters of the projects aided, are in Africa, Asia and the Americas, the balance being in the Eastern Mediterranean and Europe.

Unicef aid is given on the understanding that primary responsibility for the care of children rests on governments, while international resources are made available to supplement local efforts. The governments themselves contribute from $2 to $2.50 for each dollar provided by the Fund. Aid is confined to programmes which give promise of yielding substantial results, particularly to those related to the broader health and nutrition activities within the country, and which form part of a larger national development effort.

The Fund is governed by a 30-nation Executive Board, which meets twice a year. A government seeking Unicef assistance works out a detailed programme with representatives of the Fund and with other United Nations agencies. The proposed programme then goes to the Executive Board for approval and for an allocation of funds. The executive director of the Fund is Maurice Pate, of the United States.

Unicef's headquarters are in New York at the United Nations. Regional and area offices are situated in Paris for Europe and Africa, in Bangkok for Asia, in Beirut for the Eastern Mediterranean and in New York for the Americas. National Unicef committees exist in 19 countries to broaden and to promote public interest in the Fund and to assist in money-raising efforts.

Protection against disease

The development and improvement of permanent health and welfare services for children and mothers is Unicef's essential task. However, in many underdeveloped areas immediate protective measures against disease and steps for the improvement of standards of nutrition still have to be given priority before money and effort can be usefully spent to build up permanent services.

The fight against malaria, tuberculosis, yaws, trachoma—the major endemic diseases from which children suffer most—has not yet brought these diseases down to a level at which normal health services would be able to cope with them. Unicef provides the necessary assistance in the form of insecticide sprayers, needles and syringes, drugs and vaccines, equipment for inoculation campaigns, laboratory and clinic and medical supplies, health education material. This year more than 15 million children are being protected against tuberculosis with BCG vaccine supplied by Unicef.

The vast majority of the world's children are undernourished. The Fund has supplied milk to millions of children who have practically never known it. It has provided machinery and equipment for milk dairies and milk-drying plants to many countries, with such immediate and remarkable results that many governments have decided to continue and expand dairy programmes by their own means. Where milk is not available, advice and assistance are given in co-operation with the Food and Agriculture Organization and the World Health Organization for the development and use of other high protein foods, such as fish, flour, cotton seed and sesame seed, flour and soya-bean products.

Mother and child welfare

Unicef encourages and assists governments to develop basic health and welfare services for mothers and children as an essential part of the over-all health and social services. It participates in general programmes for public education in matters affecting sanitation, health and nutrition.

Wherever possible Unicef helps in training local personnel to overcome the shortage of trained staff—midwives, nurses, nutrition workers, sanitarians, etc.—which is the chief obstacle to progress. Equipment and medical supplies have been provided to more than 22,000 maternal and child welfare centres in rural areas and almost 26,000 centres distributed milk and vitamins and soap provided by Unicef in 1959.

The possibility is now being explored of extending the Fund's action to assist in primary education, with the co-operation of Unesco.

THE OFFICE OF THE HIGH COMMISSIONER FOR REFUGEES (UNHCR)

One of the most painful problems created by the two world wars and the political changes of our century, and one that cannot be solved without concerted international action, is that of refugees. The League of Nations had already instituted international action for the refugees, providing legal and political protection for them. This was done in order to assist them in overcoming the difficulties arising from loss of nationality and national protection, to assure them an internationally recognized legal status and to enable them to obtain travel documents.

As soon as it was established, the United Nations had to face a refugee problem far exceeding in magnitude that of the League of Nations. Over 1 million of the war-displaced persons in Europe needed international assistance in order to re-establish themselves when the emergency campaign of the United Nations Relief and Rehabilitation Administration (UNRRA) came to an end in July 1947. The International Refugee Organization (IRO), set up at the second session of the General Assembly, became responsible not only for affording legal protection but also for the care and maintenance, voluntary repatriation, resettlement, and integration of this mass of refugees.

The operations of IRO were brought to a close at the end of 1951, after it had resettled more than a million persons in new homes throughout the world and had repatriated more than 70,000.

However, the Assembly, recognizing the responsibility of the United Nations for international protection of the refugees after the termination of IRO, decided to establish the Office of the High Commissioner for Refugees (UNHCR) for a three-year term as from 1 January 1951. His mandate has since been extended twice. The present mandate expires at the end of 1963.

A refugee under UNHCR mandate is defined in the Statute of the Office as a person who, owing to a well-founded fear of persecution for reasons of race, religion, nationality or political opinion, is outside his country of origin and is unable or unwilling to avail himself of the protection of that country. Refugees, such as those in India and Pakistan, and Germans from the East of Europe, who have been given full rights of citizenship by their countries of residence, are outside the mandate. The Arab refugees from Palestine are looked after by a special United Nations agency, the United Nations Relief and Works Agency (UNRWA).

The humanitarian and social tasks—entirely non-political—of the Office of the High Commissioner for Refugees are to provide refugees with international protection, to promote permanent solutions to their problems through voluntary repatriation or their assimilation within new national communities. The administrative expenses of the Office of the High Commissioner are financed through voluntary contributions from governmental and private sources. The programmes are authorized by an Executive Committee comprising 25 members.

The High Commissioner for Refugees has headquarters at the Palais des Nations in Geneva. Dr. Auguste Lindt, of Switzerland, is the High Commissioner. Fifteen branch offices and seven correspondents maintain contact with governments of countries with refugee populations.

International protection is a basic function of UNHCR and applies to all refugees coming within its mandate. Its objective is to safeguard the legitimate interests of refugees and improve their legal position so as to put them as nearly as possible on a similar footing with nationals of the country in which they reside. In order to reach this objective UNHCR promotes the conclusion of international legal instruments concerning the rights of refugees and the adoption by individual governments of legal measures for the improvement of their status. Another activity in the field of protection consists in determining whether a person is a refugee. On this determination of eligibility depends the enjoyment of rights under the international conventions or national legislation, and even the right of asylum.

The most important international instrument for the protection of refugees is the 1951 Convention relating to the Status of Refugees. It codifies provisions included in previous instruments concerning refugees and sets out minimum rights for them, including the right to work, to social security and public assistance, and to freedom of movement within contracting States.

There are more than 900,000 refugees in Europe, and about half a million in other parts of the world under the mandate of the High Commissioner for Refugees. No solution—repatriation, emigration or integration—has yet been found for some 115,000, many of them in camps in various countries. Many are in the category of 'handicapped cases', including elderly or sick people who cannot fend for themselves.

The High Commissioner for Refugees is now successfully engaged on a plan to clear the camps in Europe. Many of the inhabitants have been living in the camps for 10 years or more. The majority could become integrated in the countries where the camps are situated.

From the beginning of 1952 until June 1960, 14,188 refugees of European origin have been resettled from the Far East via Hong Kong under the joint operation carried out between UNHCR and the Intergovernmental Committee for European Migration (ICEM). These are refugees from the USSR who have been stranded for years in China. A campaign is now in progress to resettle the remaining 8,000, many of whom have visa assurances.

In Morocco and Tunis, approximately 200,000 refugees from Algeria are receiving relief assistance under a joint operation of the High Commissioner and the League of Red Cross Societies. Chinese refugees in Hong Kong—more than 1 million of them—who came from the People's Republic of China, do not fall within the mandate of the High Commissioner. However, the General Assembly, in 1959, authorized the High Commissioner to use his good offices to encourage arrangements for contributions to assist these refugees.

Many international non-governmental organizations which take an active interest in the refugee problem, and whose collaboration with the Office of the High Commissioner for Refugees is particularly close and fruitful, are represented on the Standing Conference of Voluntary Agencies Working for Refugees. The High Commissioner's programmes of material assistance to provide permanent solutions for refugees are implemented by the voluntary agencies in co-operation with the host governments which make substantial supporting contributions. By 31 December 1960 some 39,000 refugees had been permanently settled under the programmes carried out by the Office of the High Commissioner.

In 1958 the General Assembly initiated a World Refugee Year, which began in June 1959. This was a world-wide effort to help resolve the refugee problem. It had two aims: first, to focus interest on the problem and to encourage additional financial contributions from governments, voluntary agencies and the general public; and second, to find additional opportunities for permanent solutions. Ninety-two countries and territories participated in the campaign. As of 30 June 1960, $15 million had been pledged by governments to World Refugee Year, in addition to their annual contributions for refugee purposes.

Hungarian refugees

A separate chapter in the activities of the High Commissioner for Refugees was the emergency campaign to assist more than 200,000 persons who crossed the border from Hungary into Austria and Yugoslavia in the weeks that followed the events in Hungary in November 1956.

As soon as the refugees started fleeing across the Austrian frontier, the High Commissioner for Refugees was asked by the Assembly to co-ordinate the operations of relief assistance and of resettlement. The League of Red Cross Societies and many other voluntary agencies organized the emergency relief action of feeding, clothing, finding shelter and medical care. The movement of the refugees from overcrowded camps to other countries was in the hands of the Intergovernmental Committee for European Migration (ICEM). Many governments participated in the action. In a very short time 90 per cent of the refugees had been restored to normal life in 34 countries. In the middle of 1959 all but a few thousand had found a new life, half of them in overseas countries—Australia, Canada, the United States. With a few exceptions the Hungarians adapted themselves quickly to life in new lands. Most of them are proving a definite asset to their countries of adoption.

UNITED NATIONS RELIEF AND WORKS AGENCY
FOR PALESTINE REFUGEES IN THE NEAR EAST (UNRWA)

During the course of the Israeli-Arab war of 1948 a great majority of the Arab population of the area occupied by Israeli forces abandoned their farms and houses and fled to neighbouring countries. Nearly half a million went to Jordan, thereby almost doubling its population. Two hundred thousand found refuge in the Gaza Strip, outnumbering the local population. Another hundred thousand crossed to Syria and the same number to Lebanon.

In the absence of any permanent solution, UNRWA was created by the Assembly to carry out relief and work projects for these refugees in collaboration with local governments. The mandate of the Agency, which was to expire at the end of June 1960, has been extended by the Assembly for an additional three years. At each session the Assembly is faced with urgent pleas for adequate funds to finance the Agency's work.

The Israel Government opposes repatriation of the refugees and has offered to pay compensation under certain conditions for abandoned Arab property. On the other hand, the Arab countries, hosts to the refugees, oppose plans for permanent resettlement and integration outside Israel and insist on the right of the refugees to be repatriated. The refugees themselves remain sceptical of large projects of self-support, which they tend to regard as abandonment of repatriation. In the circumstances, relief and welfare remain the main activities of UNRWA.

Basic rations of a value approximating 1,600 calories are daily distributed to some 450,000 people. Pregnant and nursing women receive additional rations. The majority of the refugees live in the Agency's camps. Health services include hospitals and dispensaries, maternity wards, vaccinations. Particular attention is paid to sanitation and water supply. More than 100,000 children attend schools maintained by the Agency. Stress is laid on vocational training.

In view of the precarious situation of the Agency, the Assembly has once more drawn attention to the fact that after 11 years the refugees have not yet been repatriated or compensated and no progress has been made in reintegrating them into the economic life of the region.

NARCOTIC DRUGS

Drug addiction and the illicit traffic which supplies the addict are now a more serious problem than they were when the League of Nations established the permanent Central Opium Board in 1925 to supervise the observance of treaties concerning drug control. Progress was made then in the manufacture of synthetic drugs for the benefit of the sick, but these drugs are channelled into illicit markets, supplementing and replacing opium and its derivatives. The volume of illicit traffic, in so far as it is reflected in seizures, has not diminished. The machinery for international control of the legitimate trade in narcotics, and for combating the illicit traffic, must be constantly overhauled and perfected to keep pace with the extension of the traffic, which is also internationally organized and has at its disposal the most up-to-date means of transportation and communication.

The United Nations leads a world campaign for the elimination of drug addiction—through international control of legitimate trade, through concerted action against illicit traffic and also through studying methods of treating addicts and restoring them to normal life.

The Commission of Narcotic Drugs, a functional body of Ecosoc, has prepared for the consideration of governments a draft of a single Convention on Drugs which will replace the existing multilateral treaties in the field of narcotics. It will extend full international control to the

raw materials of drugs (opium, poppy straw, coca leaves, cannabis); will outlaw the non-medical use of narcotics; will place under control the manufacture of new synthetic drugs. An International Narcotic Commission, a policy-making organ, and an International Control Board of experts would serve to supervise the enforcement of the convention. The present Opium Board and other supervisory organs will cease to exist. A conference of plenipotentiaries to adopt the convention will be convened in Geneva in September 1960.

In the race between growing effectiveness of control over the legal channels for the international trade in drugs, and the highly organized illicit traffic, nearly 1,300 seizures were made in the year ending May 1958. All the seizure reports are circulated to United Nations Member States with lists of persons, places, merchant ships and other means of transportation involved. Governments also receive lists of merchant seamen and members of aircrews convicted of narcotic offences. Close contact is maintained with the International Criminal Police Organization (Interpol).

The United Nations Narcotic Laboratory in Geneva has a collection of authenticated samples of opium from a number of countries, and is able to compare them with samples from seizures, and thus to determine the geographical origin of opium. This allows the channels used by traffickers to be traced, as well as leakages in the control system.

Technical assistance is provided to requesting countries to help them control narcotic drugs.

Course VI

TECHNICAL ASSISTANCE

The disparity of wealth and welfare between the nations, and the demands of the underdeveloped nations in the economic and social field, are problems which constitute a major challenge to the United Nations, in view of the principles embodied in Article 55 of the Charter. Half of mankind lives just above the starvation level. Every day there are 125,000 additional mouths to feed in a world where agriculture does not as yet keep pace with the growth of population. More than half of the world's population is illiterate, not earning enough to subsist on, and with a life expectancy of no more than 30 years.

One of the goals which the United Nations has set itself is to aid the underdeveloped countries in overcoming the immense obstacles on their road to a decent human standard of living, and to lay the basis for economic and social progress. All mankind should share the resources of the earth; poverty in one area is the concern of all; technical skill and industrial experience is a common good and should be made available to those who need it and ask for it.

Thus the United Nations technical assistance programme came into being.

As early as March 1947, action was taken by the Economic and Social Council to provide United Nations technical assistance for the economic development of the countries which needed it. The Council asked for special machinery to be established within the Secretariat to and countries in their struggle for economic and social progress, in close co-operation with the Specialized Agencies. In 1948 a first survey mission was sent to Haiti to study the needs of that country and to suggest how economic and social standards could be improved with United Nations aid. The report of that mission was discussed at the 1948 Assembly and a resolution was adopted formulating the principles of technical assistance.

A small budget of some $300,000 was allotted to provide the necessary services: international teams of experts, fellowships for the training abroad of specialists from the underdeveloped countries, training of technicians in these countries by visiting experts, aid in organizing technical institutes, and help to governments in obtaining personnel, equipment and other services for their own programmes of training.

This small experimental programme, which a year later was placed on a continuing basis, gave birth to the larger Expanded Programme of Technical Assistance of the United Nations and the Specialized Agencies, worked out by the Economic and Social Council in the summer of 1949, and unanimously approved by the Assembly in November of that year.

THE GUIDING PRINCIPLES OF TECHNICAL ASSISTANCE

The primary objective of technical assistance, as stated in the 'Observations and guiding principles' of the Ecosoc resolution, is to assist underdeveloped countries to 'strengthen their national economy through the development of their industries and agriculture, with a view to promoting their economic and political independence in the spirit of the Charter of the United Nations, and to ensure the attainment of higher levels of economic and social welfare for their entire populations'. This aid is to be given only at the request of governments, within the framework of their national or regional programmes of development, and it is to be given in the form, as far as possible, in which the recipient countries prefer to receive it. Close co-operation between the recipient government and the United Nations is essential for the success of any technical assistance mission in any country. It is vital in the execution of any programme to arouse the interest and to enlist the co-operation of the peoples of the countries concerned—not merely of their governments. With popular support, this policy of 'help them to help themselves' ought to become part of the daily, normal life of the peoples.

The 'guiding principles' also laid down that the participating organizations should avoid 'distinction arising from the political structure of the country requesting assistance, or from the race or religion of its population'. Technical assistance cannot be a means of economic or political interference nor can it be accompanied by any political considerations.

COUNTRY PROGRAMMING

In the light of experience acquired during the first few years of the programme, a system of country programming was established in 1954. This placed the responsibility for fixing technical assistance priorities on the shoulders of the requesting governments, and improved the collaboration of the governments with the technical assistance administration, which is the basic principle of the programme. It marked the trend away from piecemeal programming towards integration with the development plans of the countries concerned, and it enabled countries to take a more active part in the preparation of programmes and to build co-ordinating machinery.

Recipient countries give all the necessary information concerning the programmes and define in advance the nature and scope of the problems which they require assistance to solve. They give information on what other technical assistance they receive from other sources. They also defray in local currency a substantial part of the costs of the services they obtain; e.g., the subsistence allowance of the experts, maintenance costs of buildings used as training centres. In addition to setting up national co-ordination machinery for co-operation with technical assistance, they provide information and other material for study and analysis of the results achieved, and give publicity to the programmes in their countries. In many places special national committees have been created for these purposes.

Special attention is paid to arrangements made by recipient governments for providing counterpart personnel and for administrative support, these being essential elements in the execution of many programmes and in their eventual take-over by national authorities.

For 1961–62 it was decided to introduce two-year programming on an experimental basis. This will improve advance planning of projects and will increase efficiency in carrying them out.

The Expanded Programme provides a world-wide reservoir of skill and knowledge which may be drawn from every nation which is a member of at least one of the participating organizations—of the United Nations and the Specialized Agencies. It is, in a sense, a co-operative programme of mutual aid. All nations participate according to their capacity, and all are entitled to technical assistance services and can benefit from the work of helping each other.

FINANCING OF TECHNICAL ASSISTANCE ACTIVITIES

The Expanded Programme is financed from voluntary contributions by governments. Pledges are announced at a conference called for this purpose annually, usually in the course of the General Assembly of the United Nations. At the pledging conference for 1960 the sum of $32.6 million has so far been promised by 79 countries, with more pledges to come. By the end of 1960 a total of $268 million will have been contributed. A sum of $12 million had been set aside from these contributions by the end of 1956 as working capital and as a reserve fund to ensure financial stability and funds to carry over projects from one year to another in the case of delays in government payments. Financing is still on an annual basis; but several governments, admitting the need for long-term planning, have indicated their financial support for a period of several years.

ASSISTANCE DISTRIBUTED

During the years 1950 to 1959, 140 countries and territories requested and received technical assistance help. The majority were countries with an estimated *per capita* national income of less than the local equivalent of $150. Geographically, the assistance was as follows:

Region	Countries assisted	Percentage of total assistance	Region	Countries assisted	Percentage of total assistance
Africa	35	9.5	Latin America	35	27.2
Asia and the			Middle East	11	20.3
Far East	41	32.4	Inter-regional	—	2.8
Europe	18	7.8			

The media of technical assistance are: experts, fellowships, supplies and equipment. Of the total of $182 million spent directly on projects in 1950–59, some 71 per cent was allocated to services of international experts, 18 per cent to awards of fellowships, and 11 per cent to provision of equipment. Since the inception of the Programme some 9,000 persons have served all over the world as experts, and more than 16,000 fellowships have been awarded for study abroad.

In the early years the majority of experts came from a few industrialized countries: the proportion of United States, United Kingdom and French experts, however, has been reduced in the last 10 years from half to only one-third of the total. Experts are now recruited from 77 countries. Similar development may be noted as regards training facilities for fellowship-holders. The number of countries increased from 45 in 1951 to over 100 in 1959. The technical knowledge, experience and training facilities of many underdeveloped countries have proved an important asset for technical assistance.

THE SPECIAL FUND

It should be stressed that the technical assistance programme is not intended to provide capital for economic development. The problem of financing the economic and social progress of the underdeveloped areas has been the subject of numerous studies by United Nations experts ever since the organization began to deal with the question of under-development. A majority of members agreed to create the Special Fund for Economic Development (SUNFED) but the major industrial countries do not approve of it in present circumstances.[1]

On the other hand, the extension of technical assistance led to increased awareness of the need for financing numerous projects for which technical assistance paved the way. A compromise decision was reached: to establish a Special Fund as an extension of the existing technical assistance and development activities of the United Nations and the Specialized Agencies. The essential difference between SUNFED and the Special Fund is that whereas SUNFED would itself provide capital for development, one of the main objectives of the Special Fund is to facilitate the inflow of development capital. It does this by assisting or initiating such projects as resource surveys, applied research and vocational and advanced technical training. It carries United Nations assistance a step forward, concentrating on relatively large projects which will open the way to fruitful investment.

The Special Fund was inaugurated on 1 January 1959 with Paul G. Hoffman (United States) as Managing Director, assisted by a Governing Council.

During the first year the Fund granted over $31 million for 44 projects to speed economic progress in 50 of the underdeveloped countries and territories in Africa, Asia and Latin America. But it shares rather than bears all the costs; it requires maximum self-help on the part of the recipient countries. In carrying out the 44 approved projects, the latter will contribute $44 million out of a total of $75 million.

In presenting his first report to Ecosoc the Managing Director of the Fund pointed out that the first need of the less-developed countries is for much more knowledge to be available of their natural resources—involving surveys of mineral riches, soil content, industrial potentialities —and of their human resources. The Fund carries the work of technical assistance a step forward into the special fields suitable for capital investment, by carrying out projects which aim to create conditions for fruitful investment. He appealed for the Fund to be brought to an estimated $100 million.

HOW TECHNICAL ASSISTANCE FUNCTIONS

As already mentioned, three major forms of technical assistance are provided:
1. Technically qualified experts are sent out at the request of the governments of the countries which ask aid, to advise governments

---

1. See Course IV, 'Economic and social problems'.

and train local staff. In selecting the experts a combination of skills and moral qualities has to be looked for. A technical assistance expert is described as a person not only highly qualified in his specific job, but also versatile, adaptable to different conditions, able to impart advice without seeming to do so, and with didactic gifts. He must also be *persona grata* with the government of the country he is sent to. No expert is appointed without the approval of the government concerned.

Experts are required to give advice on subjects ranging from flood control to budget balancing, from bridge building to fish culture, from plastic production to running a news agency. A substantial number of specialists were found in the less-developed countries. For example, as many experts were recruited in India or Chile as were sent to those countries.

2. Fellowships and scholarships are granted to enable nationals of requesting countries to study methods in other lands. This is often arranged in conjunction with the sending of experts. Technicians and specialists in various fields are thus helped to keep abreast of the advances in other countries, to extend their knowledge and to adapt it to conditions in their own countries. Fellows and scholars are selected from nominees of governments requesting this form of aid.

The range of these studies is as wide as the range of expert aid: medical officials study the rehabilitation of the blind and crippled, teachers learn modern techniques of adult education, farming engineers see how to improve output in montainous areas, fiscal officers how to administer tax systems, meteorologists how to establish weather forecasting services.

Another form of assistance is the organizaion of training centres and seminars on a national or regional basis. These afford a convenient means of gathering together groups of fellows to whom experts may be brought from abroad. This is more economical than individual voyages, and enables a larger turnover of participants.

3. Equipment is supplied on a limited scale in connexion with the work of the experts, for demonstration purposes.

THE ADMINISTRATION OF TECHNICAL ASSISTANCE

The machinery for the operation of the Expanded Programme consists of a Technical Assistance Board (TAB) and a Technical Assistance Committee (TAC). The heads of the participating organizations—United Nations, ILO, FAO, Unesco, ICAO, WHO, ITU, WMO, IAEA—are members of the Board, presided over by the Executive Chairman, appointed by the United Nations Secretary General. The Fund and Bank as well as Unicef co-operate with the TAB to co-ordinate their assistance activities with those of the Expanded Programme, but do not receive any allotments from technical assistance funds.

The TAB is the co-ordinating and supervising body of all operations under the Expanded Programme and it submits its annual reports to the Technical Assistance Committee, together with plans for the coming period based on requests from the governments.

As from 1952, the TAB has found it necessary to establish a network of its own field offices in countries where the volume of assistance given requires direct and permanent liaison between the Board, the participating organizations, and the governments. These offices are headed by TAB resident representatives, whose main job is to assist governments in drawing up requests for annual programmes. They also help to evaluate the programme; render administrative assistance to TA experts; and keep the TAB informed of the progress of the programme.

Forty-one offices headed by resident representatives of the Board or by liaison officers now cover 90 per cent of the field programme.

EVALUATION OF WORK DONE

The Expanded Programme is examined every year in the course of the summer session of Ecosoc on the basis of annual reports of the TAB to the TAC, a standing organ of Ecosoc.

The programme is now 10 years old and it is possible to evaluate its role in the world's economic life, its importance and its results; the more so because, after a financial crisis caused by uncertainty of contributions in 1954–55, it has been stabilized both financially and administratively. The programme is, of course, modest and the aid small compared with the immense needs of the underdeveloped countries. Taken singly many of the projects may not amount to a great deal, but cumulatively, year after year, much is certainly being accomplished. As an international venture in co-operation, with great appeal and motive power, United Nations technical assistance is becoming an increasingly important factor in the economic and social progress of the world.

UNITED NATIONS WORK IN THE FIELD
OF TECHNICAL ASSISTANCE

To conclude, here are a few details about the direct activities of the United Nations in the field of technical assistance (details about the work of the Specialized Agencies in this connexion will be found in the respective courses on individual agencies).

The United Nations Commissioner for Technical Assistance is responsible for all assistance not specifically covered by any of the existing

Specialized Agencies, this being mainly in the fields of social welfare, economic development, public administration and human rights.

A new sphere of action was opened by the decision of the Assembly to authorize the Secretary General to assist governments which request, on a temporary basis, the services of qualified persons to perform duties of an executive and operational character. The aim is to give immediate help to improve administrative practices and to train nationals to assume responsibilities. Such nationals are assigned temporarily to these international officials. The latter do not act, however, as advisers, but as operators under the direction of the requesting national governments which cover a major part of the expense of employing the experts.

In the first year of operation of OPEX (abbreviation for 'operational and executive personnel') nine experts were appointed—including a bank manager in Nepal, an air traffic controller in Tunisia, a radio general manager in Jamaica—with 20 under consideration. Ninety requests were received from 28 countries.

Finally, it should be noted that the United Nations and the Specialized Agencies are not the only international channels for technical assistance. Several regional organizations outside the United Nations provide it, such as the Council for Technical Co-operation in South and South-East Asia (known as the Colombo Plan) and the Organization of American States. The United States has its own foreign aid programme.

To avoid duplication of effort and to utilize existing facilities to the best advantage, Ecosoc has made provision for contacts and co-operation with other technical assistance programmes.

BIBLIOGRAPHY

I saw technical assistance change lives. New York, United Nations Department of Public Information, 1957. Witness reports. Department of Public Information publications on technical assistance of preceding years are mostly out of date.

Reports of the Technical Assistance Board. These are published annually. Ten reports have been issued as supplements to Ecosoc documents.

Technical assistance for economic development. Plan for an expanded co-operative programme through the United Nations and the Specialized Agencies. Report prepared by the Secretary General in consultation with the executive heads of the interested Specialized Agencies. New York, United Nations, 1949, Document II.B.1. This document formed the basis for the debates of Ecosoc which resulted in the adoption of resolutions establishing the Expanded Programme of Technical Assistance.

Technical assistance for economic development through the United Nations and the Specialized Agencies. New York, United Nations, 1948. Document II.B.2.

Technical assistance: why, what, how. 1958. 64 pp. illus.
Women and technical assistance, illustr., 77 p.
Basic resolutions
Economic development of underdeveloped countries. Ecosoc resolutions 222
(IX) of 14 and 15 August 1949.
Observations on and guiding principles of an expanded programme of technical
assistance for economic development. Annex I to Ecosoc resolutions 222 (IX).
Expanded programme of technical assistance for the economic development
of underdeveloped countries. Annex II to Ecosoc resolutions 222 (IX).

Course VII

THE TRUSTEESHIP SYSTEM
NON-SELF-GOVERNING TERRITORIES

The well-being and progress of millions of people who live in dependent areas, who do not govern themselves and are administered by outside powers are of particular concern to the United Nations. Under the Charter, in a 'Declaration regarding non-self-governing territories' (Chapter XI), Member States administering territories whose people have not attained a full measure of self-government, have accepted, as a 'sacred trust', the obligation to promote to the utmost the well-being of the inhabitants of these areas, to ensure their political, economic, social and educational advancement, to develop self-government, and to assist in the development of their free political institutions.

The declaration goes beyond any previous international agreement concerning non-self-governing areas. It applies to territories of all Member States of the United Nations: the Charter provides for international supervision of territories under United Nations trusteeship, and what may be termed international accountability for all other non-self-governing countries.

BASIC OBJECTIVES

The basic objectives of the trusteeship system are defined in Chapter XIII of the Charter: the system shall further international peace and security; it shall promote the advancement of the inhabitants of the trust territories and their development towards self-government or independence, taking into consideration the freely expressed wishes of the peoples concerned; it shall encourage respect for basic human rights and for fundamental freedom, as well as recognition of the interdependence of the peoples of the world.

The trusteeship system applies to territories placed under it by means of trusteeship agreements: territories formerly under the mandate of the

League of Nations, those detached from enemy States as a result of the second world war, and territories voluntarily placed under the system by States responsible for their administration. An agreement submitted by the administering Member State requires the approval of the General Assembly: it defines the terms under which the territory is to be administered and designates the authority to administer the area, which can be the administering power itself, or one or more States, or the United Nations itself.

The terms of the agreement include the obligation to administer the territory in such a way as to achieve the basic objectives of trusteeship as defined in the Charter. The trusteeship agreement may designate all or a part of a territory as 'strategic', and in this case it is approved by the Security Council which exercises the United Nations responsibility in respect of such an area.

THE TRUST TERRITORIES

Of the three categories listed in the Charter, only two, in fact, have come under the trusteeship system: those held previously under the League's mandate, which had not become independent States, and territories detached from enemy States after the second world war.

Eleven territories came under trusteeship, as shown below:

Territory	Administering authority	Population	Area in square miles
Cameroons	United Kingdom	1 400 000	34 081
Togoland	United Kingdom	410 000	13 040
Tanganyika	United Kingdom	7 950 000	362 688
Cameroons	France	3 100 000	166 797
Togoland	France	1 000 000	21 236
Ruanda-Urundi	Belgium	4 100 000	20 916
Somaliland	Italy	1 250 000	194 000
Western Samoa	New Zealand	85 000	1 133
Nauru	Australia	3 250	82
New Guinea	Australia	1 100 000	93 000
Pacific Islands	United States	60 000	687

The former Italian colony of Somaliland was added to the original list by a decision of the General Assembly in November 1949 for a period of 10 years pending independence as a sovereign State, and Italy was designated as the administering authority during that period.

The trust territories of the Pacific Islands under United States administration have been designated as strategic areas.

THE TRUSTEESHIP COUNCIL

The system is administered by the Trusteeship Council under the authority of the General Assembly. The Council consists of Member States administering trust territories, of permanent members of the Security Council who do not administer such areas, and of as many non-administering members (elected for three years by the Assembly) as will assure that membership is equally divided between those members administering trust territories and those which do not.

The Council exercises its function of supervising the administration of the trust territories by considering reports from administering authorities, by accepting petitions relating to the territories and examining them with the administering authorities, and by periodic visits to the trust territories. The Council normally meets twice a year. Decisions are taken by simple majority of members present and voting.

ANNUAL REPORTS

The reports submitted by the administering authorities present a comprehensive picture of the political, economic, social and educational progress of a trust territory, and deal with a multitude of questions, ranging from the development of political parties and the construction of water pipelines to the difficulties in combating polygamy. Recommendations are formulated by the Trusteeship Council after it has examined conditions in the territory. A representative of the administering authority is present at this examination.

PETITIONS

The examination of petitions from the territories is another major task of the Council. Any man or woman or group of individuals has the right to address grievances or demands directly to the United Nations. Thousands of people, individually or jointly, have exercised this right.

The petitions concern a variety of subjects, from organized protests and requests about political and economic conditions of the territories to such individual demands and complaints as that of a donkey-car driver in Somaliland about high taxation or another from women in the Pacific Islands about the need to induce their men-folk to consume less strong drink. Each petition is sympathetically examined by the Council and an answer is sent to the petitioner.

In some instances the Council has heard the petitioners themselves present their cases orally. This was the case with the petition of the Western Samoans for self-government. A Council mission went to the islands to examine the situation and to discuss it with Samoan leaders.

Subsequent developments led to an agreement concluded in 1956 between the Government of New Zealand and the representative institutions of the territory for a series of constitutional reforms which would give Western Samoans a cabinet system of government in 1960.

VISITING MISSIONS TO TRUST TERRITORIES

Since 1947 each territory has been visited three or four times. A mission consists normally of four members—two representatives of administering members and two of non-administering powers, usually appointed from the members of the Council.

The missions visit schools and hospitals, inspect public utilities and industrial plants, confer with tribal chiefs and talk to ordinary people and receive petitions. The reports of the visiting missions are a most valuable addition to information received from other sources on progress and developments in the trust territories.

FROM TRUSTEESHIP TO STATEHOOD AND INDEPENDENCE

The proof of the effectiveness of the trusteeship system lies in the fact that five of the trust territories have reached or are reaching statehood and independence.

Since the ultimate aim of trusteeship is to end it, the General Assembly, on 13 December 1956, with great satisfaction took its first decision of this kind—that of terminating the trusteeship agreement for British Togoland. The population of that territory, in the plebiscite held under United Nations supervision in May 1956, voted by 58 per cent in favour of union with the independent Ghana State, and it became a part of the new free country—the first trust territory where the goal of the Charter was reached.

The 1958 Assembly took cognizance of the fact that France and the Republic of Togo agreed to the independence of that territory in April 1960. The trusteeship agreement with France was then to come to an end.

In March 1959 the General Assembly voted to end the trusteeship of another African territory, the Cameroons under French administration. By 1 January 1960 the Cameroons was an independent State.

For the Cameroons administered by the United Kingdom, a plebiscite will be held in the northern part before March 1961, to decide whether it will join Nigeria or the former French Cameroons, now the Cameroons Republic. In the southern part another plebiscite will be held to vote on its future.

In East Africa, Somaliland is already enjoying a large measure of internal autonomy, pending the granting of independence in 1960.

At its fourteenth session the General Assembly expressed the wish to see a time limit set for the achievement of self-government in Tanganyika and Ruanda-Urundi in East Africa. In the Pacific area where the four remaining trust territories lie, special interest is taken in speedy establishment of cabinet government in Western Samoa, and in the future of the Nauruan people, pending the proclamation of independence in 1961.

THE CASE OF SOUTH WEST AFRICA

One of the former mandated territories has not yet been brought within the trusteeship system. This is South West Africa which the Union of South Africa had refused to place under trusteeship. The Union holds that in view of the lapsing of the League of Nations mandate which had been exercised by the Union over former German South West Africa, South Africa had no legal obligation to negotiate with the United Nations on that territory.

The International Court of Justice, ruling on the Assembly's request for an advisory opinion, found unanimously, in July 1950, that the Union continued to have international obligations under the League's mandate, including the obligation to transmit petitions from the territory, but had no legal obligation to place the territory under trusteeship. The Union was not, however, qualified to modify the territory's international status unilaterally, without the consent of the United Nations. The Union continued to refuse to recognize United Nations competence in this matter.

The Assembly, on the other hand, proceeded to study the situation and established a Committee on South West Africa to report on conditions in that area. The committee presented several reports on the unsatisfactory conditions in the territory: its report in 1956 stated that the main efforts in administering the territory were directed almost exclusively in favour of the European minority, often at the expense of the African population. The problem is a recurrent item on the agenda of the General Assembly, which has repeated almost every year its decision to place the territory under the trusteeship system.

NON-SELF-GOVERNING TERRITORIES

The 'Declaration regarding non-self-governing territories' in Chapter XI of the Charter established the important principle that Member States with dependent areas are accountable to the United Nations, and that the well-being of their inhabitants is a matter of vital international concern. The operative part of the declaration is Article 73(e) of the Charter, which provides that administering members should agree to

transmit regularly to the Secretary General statistical and other information relating to economic, social and educational conditions in the
territories for which they are responsible.

Many more territories and a much larger population fell within the
category of 'non-self-governing' than within that of trust territories. In
1946 eight Member States indicated that they would send information
to the United Nations on 74 territories with a population of approximately 215 million. Many of these have since attained self-government,
fulfilling the conditions under which the provisions of Chapter XI cease
to apply. Indonesia, Indo-China (Laos, Cambodia), the Gold Coast
(Ghana), Malaya, Tunisia, Morocco and Guinea have become independent States and members of the United Nations.

Information on the situation in the territories is transmitted annually
to the Secretary General. It is summarized, analysed and classified by
the Secretariat for examination by a special Committee on Information
from Non-self-governing Territories. Information is given on social,
economic and educational conditions, on government, population trends,
and civil rights. Information concerning government of a territory is
optional. Data are requested on the extent to which the indigenous
populations participate in territorial and local government. Administering
members are invited to submit surveys of measures for economic and
social advancement, including the use of technical assistance.

Having discussed the information presented, the committee formulates
its recommendations. Such recommendations, in the economic field,
have expressed the view that development plans should, in the first place,
serve to alleviate poverty and raise the standard of living of the population; that conservation of natural resources of the territories is an essential condition of agricultural development in order to secure an adequate
food supply; and that industrial development should secure a higher
proportion of profits to the population. In many of these territories,
United Nations technical assistance is active.

As to social conditions, stress has been laid on the importance of
popular participation in planning and executing programmes of social
advancement, and training of native personnel for social services to meet
local needs. The necessity of strengthening trade union activities has
been emphasized. Abolition of discrimination has been repeatedly
recommended. Problems of public health, of training and recruitment of
personnel for health services, and questions of nutrition and of feeding
of children have been reviewed in co-operation with WHO and FAO.

As regards education, the view has been recorded that primary
education should gradually become free and compulsory and that
secondary education should provide specialized knowledge and training.
The development of universities has been urged, in view of the increasing
call for local inhabitants in industry, administration and professions.

Unesco has been invited to co-operate in drafting recommendations for the eradication of illiteracy, for teaching adults and women, on vocational training and on the use of vernacular languages in education.

FACTORS DETERMINING SELF-GOVERNMENT

As in the trusteeship system, the ultimate aim of the United Nations in dealing with the question of non-self-governing territories is to assist them to achieve full self-government. The progress of the work of the United Nations in this field is measured by the diminution in the number of dependent areas.

A procedure was established regarding cessation of the transmission of information, which is a recognition of the fact that the territory can no longer be considered as non-self-governing; and a list was drawn up of factors which determine self-government. These are: political advancement of the population to a point sufficient to enable them to decide the future destiny of the territory by means of democratic processes; functioning of a representative system of government; freedom of political life; universal suffrage; guarantee of basic rights, freedom of speech, press, assembly, religion; right to a fair trial; and absence of any pressure on the population in expressing their views as to the national or international status they desire.

Course VIII

LEGAL WORK OF THE UNITED NATIONS

Some aspects of the administration of international law have been entrusted to the United Nations with the aim of establishing 'conditions under which justice and respect for the obligations arising from treaties and other sources of international law can be maintained'. To achieve this, a judicial organ has been created in the Charter: the International Court of Justice. The General Assembly established an organ charged with the progressive development of international law and its codification: the International Law Commission. Technical and advisory legal functions are performed by the Secretariat; and, of course, the United Nations has helped to regulate international conduct by conventions in various fields of human activity, adopted by the Assembly and its technical organs, and by the work done to further observance of and respect for human rights and freedoms.

THE INTERNATIONAL COURT OF JUSTICE

The International Court of Justice is defined in the Charter as the 'principal judicial organ of the United Nations'. Its statute is an integral part of the Charter, and the Court is one of the six main organs of the United Nations.

At its first session the General Assembly elected the judges of the Court, which was thus able to start functioning at the same time as other organs of the United Nations. The Court took over the Peace Palace in The Hague, the former seat of the Permanent Court of International Justice. The judges of the Court are elected by an absolute majority of both the General Assembly and the Security Council, simultaneously but separately, from a list of persons nominated by national groups of the Permanent Court of Arbitration (a panel of jurists from which States, when they desire to submit a dispute to arbitration, may select members of a court to hear the case), or by national groups appointed for this purpose. Not more than one candidate of the same nationality may be elected, and the main forms of civilization and the principal legal systems of the world should be represented in the Court. The judges are elected for a term of nine years and can be re-elected. Every three years they choose a President and a Vice-President of the Court.

The 15 judges are permanently at the disposal of the Court and cannot exercise any other function. No judge can be dismissed unless, in the unanimous opinion of the other judges, he has ceased to fulfil the required conditions.

Functions of the secretariat of the Court are performed by its Registry, headed by a Registrar, elected by the Court. The Registry publishes the judgements of the Court, its advisory opinions, and other documents.

Parties to the Court and access to it. All members of the United Nations are *ipso facto* parties to the statute of the court. States which are non-members of the United Nations may become parties to the statute on conditions determined in each case by the General Assembly on the recommendation of the Security Council. Switzerland, Liechtenstein, San Marino and Japan (two years before her admission to the United Nations) have in this way become parties to the Court's statute. They are entitled to take part in the election of the judges in the General Assembly. The Court is also open to States which are not parties to its statute, on certain conditions laid down by the Security Council in a resolution adopted in 1946.

The Court is not open to individuals or private organizations. However, private interests can be the subject of proceedings before the Court when a State takes up the complaint of one of its nationals against another State, and puts its case before the Court with adequate procedural and legal reasons. It is then a dispute between States.

The jurisdiction of the Court comprises cases which the parties refer to it and all matters specially provided for in the Charter or in treaties and conventions. The Court's jurisdiction is optional; it depends on the consent of States, which can be given in various ways. Two States in disagreement over a certain question may agree to refer it to the Court and accept its decision; there are a great number of treaties and conventions under which States bind themselves to accept the jurisdiction of the Court. Furthermore, under the Court's statute, States may undertake to accept, in advance, the compulsory jurisdiction of the Court in certain categories of cases in relation to other States accepting the same obligation.

Laws applied, and procedure in contentious cases. The Court decides disputes submitted to it, applying international treaties and conventions, international custom, general principles of law recognized by civilized nations, judicial decisions and the teaching of the most highly qualified writers as subsidiary means for the determination of the rules of law. The Court may also decide a case *ex aequo et bono*, i.e., according to the principles of equity, if the participants agree to this.

Parties to a case are represented by agents and may have the assistance of counsel and advocates. Oral hearings are public, unless the Court decides otherwise or the parties demand that the public be excluded.

All questions are decided by a majority of judges present. The President has a casting vote. The judgement must state the reasons on which it is based and must contain the names of judges taking part in the decisions. Any judge is entitled to give a separate opinion, attached to the judgement.

The judgement is read in open court. It is final and without appeal, but a revision can be claimed on the ground of a decisive new fact which was unknown to the party and to the Court when judgement was given. A judgement is binding on the parties in the case, once they have come before the Court. If, however, any party fails to carry out the obligations under a judgement of the Court, the other party may have recourse to the Security Council, which may make recommendations or decide on measures to give effect to the judgement.

The Court also gives advisory opinions on any legal questions at the request of the General Assembly or the Security Council, or at the request of any other organ of the United Nations and the Specialized Agencies when authorized to do so by the General Assembly.

SOME CASES DEALT WITH BY THE COURT

The first case to come before the Court, the Corfu Channel case, arose from a disputee between the United Kingdom and Albania concerning damage to British warships and loss of life which, it was alleged, resulted from mines in the Corfu Channel during October 1946. The Court fixed a compensation of $844,000 to be paid to the United Kingdom, but Albania held that the Court had no jurisdiction to assess the amount of reparation and refused to pay. Albania submitted a counter-claim, accusing the United Kingdom of violating Albanian sovereignty by carrying out mine-sweeping operations in Albanian territorial waters after the explosion. The Court found that this constituted a violation of Albanian sovereignty, and that the declaration of the Court was in itself an appropriate satisfaction for Albania.

Three cases concerning the granting of asylum in the Colombian Embassy at Lima in January 1949 to the Peruvian political leader, Mr. Haya de la Torre, accused of military rebellion, went to the Court by agreement of Colombia and Peru. The Court found asylum had been granted irregularly and that on this ground Peru was entitled to ask for its termination, but it declared, at the same time, that Colombia was not bound to surrender the refugee. The two conclusions were not contradictory because there were other ways in which the asylum could be terminated. Colombia and Peru consequently agreed in direct talks that Mr. Haya de la Torre would be given safe conduct out of the Embassy and out of Peru. He left for Mexico in April 1954.

Sovereignty over two groups of tiny islets in the English Channel was decided in favour of the United Kingdom. France and Britain agreed to ask the Court which of the parties had produced a more convincing proof of the title to Minquiers and Ecrehos Islets, situated between the island of Jersey and the coast of France. Various mediaeval documents, going back to William the Conqueror, were examined by the Court, which based its judgement, however, on direct evidence of possession and the actual exercise of sovereignty.

A case in which a government took up a complaint from one of its nationals was that of the Greek shipowner Ambatielos, who sued the government of the United Kingdom for failure to carry out the terms of a contract for the purchase of ships. The Greek Government submitted the case to the Court, claiming that it was the duty of the United Kingdom to submit the dispute to arbitration in accordance with existing United Kingdom-Greek treaties. The Court proclaimed a judgement in favour of Greece.

Among its advisory opinions the Court has laid down: that the United Nations is competent to claim reparation for damage suffered by persons on mission for the organization (this case arose as a consequence of the assassination in Palestine of Count Bernadotte, the United Nations mediator); that the judgements of the United Nations Administrative Tribunal concerning non-observance of contracts of employment of staff members are binding on the United Nations and thus on the General Assembly. Other opinions have concerned interpretation of peace treaties; reservations to the Genocide convention, etc.

THE INTERNATIONAL LAW COMMISSION

Charged with promoting progressive development of international law and its codification, the International Law Commission, an organ of the General Assembly, was established in November 1947.

By progressive development of international law is meant the drafting of conventions on subjects not yet regulated by international law, or in respect of which the law is not yet sufficiently developed in the practice of States. Codification of international law consists of precise formulation and systematization of rules of international law in fields where there has already been extensive State practice, precedent and doctrine.

Members of the commission—21 of them—serve in their individual capacity as experts. The commission holds annual sessions in the European Office of the United Nations in Geneva, lasting from eight to ten weeks.

At ist first session in the spring of 1949 the commission made a survey of international law in order to select topics for codification. The progress of the commission's work is necessarily slow. Before the last stage of drafting an instrument on any given topic is reached, there must be: preliminary surveys of the law, and of practice and precedents on a given subject; the long and arduous task of the special rapporteur who prepares the first draft; a detailed debate in the commission before the revised draft is adopted; consultations with governments and study of their comments (this causes a particularly long delay); review of the governments' replies; and another debate in the commission, before the last stage of drafting is reached.

The law of the sea. Of the 14 topics selected for codification, one—that of the régime of high seas and the régime of territorial waters—has reached the stage of decision by an international conference of plenipotentiaries.

The conference met in Geneva in February-April 1958. Eighty-six States were represented. After a thorough review of the articles of the draft prepared by the commission, the conference adopted four separate conventions—a Convention on the Territorial Sea and the Contiguous Zone, a Convention on the High Sea, a Convention on Fishing and Conservation of Living Resources of the High Sea, and a Convention on the Continental Shelf.

In the Convention on the Territorial Sea and the Contiguous Zone the conference did not include any provision determining the breadth of the territoreal sea. It requested the General Assembly to convoke a second United Nations conference on the Law of the Sea for further consideration of this problem and other unsettled questions. The conference met in the spring of 1960.

The conventions have already obtained more than fifty signatures. Ratification by 22 signatories is required for any convention to enter into force.

Nationality, including statelessness. This is the subject of another draft convention which emerged from the commission in a final form for discussion by an international conference of plenipotentiaries. The draft convention aims at facilitating acquisition of the nationality of a country by those born within its borders, and avoiding the loss of nationality except when another nationality is acquired.

The conference on the subject met in Geneva in March 1959, with

32 countries represented. Serious divergence of opinion appeared on the article dealing with deprivation of nationality, and on the application of *jus soli* and *jus sanguini*. The conference adopted most of the articles of the future convention, but being 'unable to terminate in the time provided for its work', it adjourned until reconvened by a decision of the General Assembly.

The commission also prepared a draft Convention on Arbitral Procedure which has, however, been referred back to it for further study.

Definition of aggression has been under consideration by the United Nations ever since 1950, when the Assembly asked the International Law Commission to formulate its views on the subject. The commission decided to embody a general definition of aggression in a draft code of offences against the peace and security of mankind, on which it was working. Any use of armed force by one State against another for any purpose except national or collective self-defence, or in execution of United Nations decisions, would be considered to constitute aggression.

In the subsequent debates in the Assembly, opinions were divided as to the possibility, the desirability and the practical value of a definition of aggression, and the question remains open.

The code of offences against the peace and the security of mankind was drafted in 1951: it was limited to offences of a political nature which endangered or disturbed international peace, fomented civil strife, violated treaty obligations concerning armament limitations, etc. The fact that a person acted as a head of a State or as a responsible government official would not relieve him of responsibility.

In 1957 the Assembly linked this problem with the problem of defining aggression, and postponed them both indefinitely.

The commisison forwarded to the Assembly the opinion that the establishment of an International Criminal Court for the trial of genocide and certain other crimes was both possible and desirable. No action was taken by the Assembly on the subject.

The commission is now working on draft conventions on diplomatic intercourse and immunities and on the law of treaties.

GENOCIDE

Genocide—a word coined during the second world war—is a crime under international law. The General Assembly unanimously declared this to be so on 11 December 1946. Two years later it adopted without an opposing vote the Convention on Genocide, which received the largest number of ratifications of any convention adopted under the Charter.

Acts 'committed with the intent to destroy, in whole or in part, a national, ethnical, social or religious group' are punishable as genocide— such acts including the killing of members of a group, the deliberate infliction of conditions to bring about physical destruction, the imposition of measures to prevent births, and the forcible transfer of children. All offenders shall be punished, whether they are constitutionally responsible rulers, public officials, or private individuals. States adhering to the convention are required to pass the necessary laws to give effect to it and to grant extradition in cases of genocide. Those guilty of genocide are to be tried in the country where the crime was committed or by such international tribunals as may have jurisdiction.

REVIEWING THE CHARTER

At its 1953 session the Assembly asked for the appointment of a committee to consider fixing a time and a place for a general conference of all United Nations members for the purpose of reviewing the Charter in accordance with Article 109. The Secretariat prepared for the use of the committee a voluminous documentation, including a *Repertory of Practice of the United Nations*. This is a comprehensive summary in five volumes (and supplements) of the decisions of United Nations organs, presented in such a way as to throw light on the practical application and interpretation of the Charter.

The committee met in June 1957 and decided to report to the Assembly in 1959. The opinion prevailed that, while a review of the Charter was desirable, the time was not yet ripe to call a General Conference for that purpose.

REGISTRATION AND PUBLICATION OF TREATIES

The Charter provides that every treaty and international agreement concluded after the coming into force of the Charter shall be registered and published by the United Nations. A treaty cannot be invoked before the United Nations, if it has not been duly registered.

REFERENCE AND BIBLIOGRAPHY

Series V of *United Nations publications*, the catalogue of United Nations for 1945-55, and for 1955 and 1956 contains, under the heading 'International Law', a list of United Nations surveys, reports and texts of conventions on legal questions.

LISSITZYN, O. J. *The International Court of Justice: its role in the maintenance of international peace and security.* New York, Carnegie Endowment for International Peace, 1951.

The crime of genocide. New York, United Nations Department of Public Information, 1956. With the text of the convention.

The International Law Commission. New York, United Nations Department of Public Information Research Section. Background Paper No. 64.

Course IX

ADMINISTRATION OF THE UNITED NATIONS

The Assembly and all other organs of the United Nations are serviced by an internationally recruited Secretariat, headed by the Secretary General, the Chief Administrative Officer of the United Nations. His term of office is five years. The first Secretary General, Trygve Lie of Norway, whose term expired on 1 February 1951, was voted to continue in office for three more years, but resigned in November 1952. His successor, Dag Hammarskjöld of Sweden, became Secretary General on 7 April 1953, and was reappointed for a further five years in September 1957.

The Secretary General acts in that capacity personally or through his representatives at all meetings of the Assembly and the Councils. He submits annually his report to the Assembly on the progress of the work of the United Nations. He may bring to the attention of the Security Council any matter which in his opinion may threaten international peace and security.

The Secretariat is organized as follows:

Executive Office of the Secretary General, headed by Andrew W. Cordier (United States), Executive Assistant to the Secretary General.

Office of Legal Affairs; head: Constantin Stavropoulos (Greece).

Office of the Controller; head: Bruce R. Turner (New Zealand).

Office of Personnel; head: W. A. B. Hamilton (United Kingdom).

Under-Secretaries for Special Political Affairs: Ralph J. Bunche (United States), and C. V. Narasimhan (India).

Office of Public Information; acting head: Alfred G. Katzin (South Africa).

Department of Economic and Social Affairs; head: Under-Secretary Philippe de Seynes (France).

Department of Political and Security Council Affairs; head: (vacant at present).

Department of Trusteeship and Information from Non-self-governing Territories; head: Under-Secretary Dragoslav Protich (Yugoslavia).

Department of Conference Services; head: Under-Secretary Victor Hoo (China).

Offices and representatives of the United Nations and its organs are spread all over the world. In Geneva, the Palais des Nations, built for the League of Nations in 1936, houses the European Office of the United Nations, the Economic Commission for Europe, and the Office of the High Commissioner for Refugees. The network of 31 offices of the resident representatives of the Technical Assistance Board covers 50 countries; information centres are situated in 27 countries. United Nations organs dealing with Palestine questions have their seat in Jerusalem; the United Nations Relief and Works Agency is in Beirut, Lebanon; the Economic Commission for Asia and the Far East in Bangkok, Thailand; the Economic Commission for Latin America in Santiago, Chili; the Economic Commission for Africa in Addis Ababa, Ethiopia.

THE STAFF

Staff members of the United Nations are appointed by the Secretary General under regulations approved by the Assembly. On taking up their posts all staff members sign an oath of allegiance to the United Nations: they undertake, in the performance of their duties, in accordance with Article 100 of the Charter, not to seek or receive instructions from any government or any authority outside the United Nations. The Secretary General and the Under-Secretaries take the oath publicly, before the General Assembly.

Great care is taken to assure an equitable geographical distribution of staff members, although efficiency, competence and integrity are considered first in recruiting the staff.

In 1959, the staff of the United Nations consisted of 4,745 persons: 1,620 professionals, 2,490 in the General Services category, 251 in field services, and 245 manual workers. Ninety-five of the total were seconded to United Nations agencies for special assignments.

The rights and obligations of the staff are governed by staff regulations, which cover conditions of service, the classification of posts, salaries and allowances, rules concerning appointment, promotion and separation from service, leave, social security, disciplinary measures and appeals. Each staff member is provided with a booklet containing staff regulations and rules.

Staff members have the right of appeal against an administrative decision which they consider does not observe their terms of appointment, or against disciplinary action. A joint appeals board—an independent chairman, a member appointed by the Secretary General and one elected by the staff—advises the Secretary General on the appeals. Final decisions rest with the Secretary General. At a higher level, staff members can submit applications to the United Nations Administrative Tribunal alleging non-observance of the terms of their appointment or their contract.

Staff members are participants in the United Nations Joint Staff Pension Fund, created to provide retirement pensions and other benefits. Six Specialized Agencies are also members of the fund.

United Nations employees are organized in a Staff Association, whose purpose is to ensure that the staff rules are observed, to safeguard the rights and defend the interests of the staff, and to represent it before the Secretary General and the competent organs of the United Nations. Together with staff organizations of the Specialized Agencies, the United Nations Staff Association forms the Federation of International Civil Servants Associations (FICSA).

UNITED NATIONS FINANCES

For financing its work the United Nations uses the methods common to modern democratic states, with one difference: the Assembly votes estimates of expenditure and then establishes a scale of contributions for Member States to cover these expenses in full, after the deduction of a comparatively small revenue from other sources. The United Nations does not tolerate budgetary deficits and has no debts, with the exception of the residue of the $65 million loan, free of interest, for the construction of the headquarters buildings. At the end of 1960, a sum of $47.5 million will remain to be paid in annual instalments. Any emergency expenditure, not provided for by the budget, has to be approved by the Assembly and covered in the usual way, by contributions from Member States.

The Secretary General prepares the annual budgetary estimates in April-May, to be examined by the Advisory Committee on Administrative and Budgetary Questions, the financial watchdog of the United Nations. Amendments and reductions recommended by this committee usually secure the approval of the Assembly. The Advisory Committee also regularly considers the financial and auditing reports, pension fund finances, the budgets of the Specialized Agencies in relation to the United Nations budget, and questions of co-ordination and common services of the United Nations and the agencies.

For the year 1960 the Assembly voted a budget of $63,149,700 on the expenditure side, compared with $60,802,120 voted in 1959. Income in 1960 was estimated at $5,375,500.

Member States contribute to the expenses of the United Nations on a scale determined by the Assembly. This ranges from 0.04 per cent to 32.51 per cent (United States). On the same scale, a permanent Working Capital Fund has been established, which now reaches $25 million.

IMMUNITIES AND PRIVILEGES

The Charter provides that the United Nations shall enjoy such privileges and immunities as are necessary for the fulfilment of its purposes, and that representatives of Member States and officials of the Organization shall have a status allowing them an independent exercise of their functions. The Assembly approved in 1946 a General Convention on the Privileges and Immunities of the United Nations. This provides for the immunity of United Nations property and assets from all legal processes, from direct taxes and custom duties; it declares its premises inviolable, and specifies the personal privileges and immunities of the representatives of Member States and of officials of the Secretariat. It also states that the United Nations may issue 'laissez-passers' for its officials, these being recognized now as valid travel documents by a number of Member States.

By 1960, 62 Member States had acceded to the convention. A special agreement was concluded in 1947 with the United States Government on Headquarters in New York, and a parellel agreement was signed with the Swiss Government about the European Office of the United Nations.

The Assembly has also adopted an official seal and an emblem of the United Nations and has asked Member States to prohibit the use of the emblem, the name and the initials of the United Nations without the authorization of the Secretary General. A United Nations flag has also been instituted—a light blue background (United Nations blue) with the official emblem in white in the centre. The use of the flag is governed by a special code prescribing the manner in which it is to be displayed by governments, organizations, and individuals.

Practically all Member States—80 of them—have established permanent missions at the Headquarters in New York. Their credentials are submitted to the Secretary General. The permanent missions enjoy privileges and immunities similar to those of diplomatic missions.

HEADQUARTERS AND THE PALAIS DES NATIONS

The United Nations budget contains one item, ranging from $1 million to $2.5 million, which will be regularly inserted until 1982: this is the sum provided for the repayment of the $65 million loan, free of interest, granted by the United States for the construction of Headquarters, of which the United Nations took possession in June 1951. By the end of

1960, a total of $17.5 million will have been repaid to the United States.

The Headquarters is a group of four constructions: the General Assembly building, the Secretariat building, the Conference Area, and the Library. The Conference Area comprises three Council Chambers for the Security Council, Ecosoc and the Trusteeship Council, meeting-rooms for the main committees, lounges and restaurants. The buildings are equipped with all the most up-to-date installations for conference services, for simultaneous interpretation, for radio and television transmissions and for printing and reproduction.

For a small fee, a visitor to the United Nations can join one of the regular guided tours through the buildings and halls. Member States have donated the decorations of the Assembly Hall and the Council Halls, as well as numerous decorative items of high artistic value.

The Palais des Nations, the seat of the European Office, is similarly equipped. It was built in 1936 for the League of Nations and is the second largest construction in Europe. As at Headquarters many paintings and other works of art, rare woods and tapestries decorate the conference rooms and the lobbies, having been presented by various countries. The Palais des Nations can be visited throughout the year.

Both Headquarters and the European Office possess important libraries to provide information, research material and library services on United Nations and on international problems, for delegations, for the Secretariat, and for the public. At Headquarters, a new six-storey library building is now under construction, made possible through a $6.2 million grant from the Ford Foundation. It will accommodate the present 200,000 volumes with expansion possibilities to a total of 400,000 volumes. The main reading-room, including a reference service with some 10,000 volumes and reading area for some 100 persons, will also house the public catalogues designed to accommodate 2 million cards, the loan desk and the acquisition and catalogue sections. The library in Geneva is an international research centre of some 500,000 volumes and 5,000 periodicals, which are received regularly. The two libraries issue monthly lists of books catalogued by them. The Geneva library compiles a monthly selection of articles on political, economic, social and other questions.

The United Nations has also created a network of depository libraries in many countries in order to provide collections of United Nations documents and publications and make them available for research and reference. There now exist more than 200 such libraries in 80 States and territories.

Most of United Nations documents are produced in mimeographed form for the use of Member States and of the Secretariat. A great part of these are later issued in final form as United Nations publications and are sold to the public. All United Nations publications are listed in periodical catalogues. The publications are available from United Nations sales agents throughout the world; the list of the agents is printed on the cover of practically every volume.

A United Nations Postal Administration was established in 1951 on the basis of an agreement with the United States Post Office Department. This Administration operates a post office on behalf of the United Nations, using only United Nations postage stamps, supplied by United Nations free of charge. The United Nations sells the stamps for philatelic purposes only. Special stamps are issued at frequent intervals. The steadily growing revenue from the sale of stamps testifies to the great interest of collectors in United Nations stamps. In Geneva, the Swiss Post Office sells special stamps at the Palais des Nations, for official mail only.

The United Nations has its own telecommunication system. Its radio circuit links Headquarters with the radio station at the European Office, which is in communication with United Nations radio stations in Jerusalem, Rawalpindi (India) and Bangkok, which in turn provide liaison with United Nations organs and offices in a number of countries. United Nations traffic only is accepted over this network.

BIBLIOGRAPHICAL REFERENCE

PATRICK, Douglas; PATRICK, Mary. *The postage stamps and postal history of the United Nations.* Toronto, Ryerson Press, 1955. 174 pp.

Course X

CO-OPERATION WITH NON-GOVERNMENTAL ORGANIZATIONS

One of the characteristics of public life in modern times is the growth and the development of voluntary, independent organizations created by groups of people to further their common interests, to defend the principles in which they believe, to support causes dear to their hearts. In the last decades societies and organizations in various countries, pursuing common ends, have established links across frontiers and created their international centres.

Voluntary international organizations with major interests—such as religious and humanitarian work, peace, science, art, professional rights —have become an important factor in international co-operation. Representing public opinion and the interests of their national components, they speak in the name of large segments of people spread throughout the world. Despite the variety of their interests they have one thing in common: their belief in the principle of international co-operation. Many of these international non-governmental organizations— NGOs for short—have also built up efficient machinery, playing a useful part in international collaboration in many fields of human activity.

THE UNITED NATIONS CHARTER AND THE NGOS

The Charter took cognizance of the assistance which the NGOs can give the United Nations in dealing with economic, social and cultural problems. It provides, in Article 71, suitable arrangements for consultations between the Economic and Social Council and the international NGOs and, where appropriate, the national ones.

These arrangements took the form of special machinery, giving the organizations the opportunity to express their views and the Council to use special experience or technical knowledge which the NGOs possess. Most of the important world-wide organizations—such as labour federations, chambers of industry and commerce, leading welfare and social associations, co-operative societies, religious bodies, professional organizations—have been granted a consultative status with the United Nations. The list also includes international groups aiming at the furtherance of peace, or supporting the aims and the purposes of the United Nations.

Categories A and B. The register. All these organizations are divided into two categories. Ten, considered to have a basic interest in most activities of Ecosoc, are listed in category A. They are: International Chamber of Commerce, International Confederation of Free Trade Unions, International Co-operative Alliance, International Federation of Agricultural Producers, International Federation of Christian Trade Unions, World Federation of Trade Unions, International Organization of Employers, Inter-Parliamentary Union, World Federation of United Nations Associations, and World Veterans' Federation.

Category B includes organizations which have a special competence in only a few of the fields of activity covered by Ecosoc. More than 120 organizations are listed in this category.

A register is also kept of some 200 organizations, which have a contribution to make to the work of the Council, but with whom continuous consultative relationship is not considered necessary.

All matters concerning the Council's relationship with the NGOs are handled by the seven-member Standing Committee on Non-governmental Organizations. It makes recommendations concerning consultative status; it advises on hearings to be granted to organizations and on inclusion in the Council's agenda of items proposed by organizations in category A.

PURPOSE OF CONSULTATION

Consultative arrangements are designed to provide information and advice from organizations having special competence in particular fields, and to enable organizations representing important interests to express their views in the United Nations.

Organizations in all three categories may send representatives to the sessions of Ecosoc and of its commissions. Those in categories A and B may submit written statements to the Council and may make oral statements to the Council's NGO committee and to the commissions.

Category A organizations may propose items to be placed on the provisional agenda of the Council, and may support these items orally in plenary meetings of the Council. Also, on the recommendation of the NGO committee, they may speak on items not proposed by them, and propose items for the commissions.

Organizations on the register have limited rights. They may be invited by the Secretary General to submit written statements to the Council or its commissions, and in exceptional cases may be heard by the committee or commission.

NGOs may be asked to carry out specific studies or to prepare papers; to send representatives to public meetings of the General Assembly at which matters within their competence are discussed. They cannot, however, make any oral statements at meetings of the Assembly or its committees.

Facilities accorded to NGOs include distribution of appropriate documents, informal discussion on matters of special interest to them, use of the United Nations libraries, accommodation for meetings, when the NGOs discuss their relationship with the United Nations. The facilities also include working-rooms and document-counters at Headquarters and in Geneva.

EFFECTS OF THE CO-OPERATION

The NGOs make full use of their rights and facilities. Among items included on the agenda of Ecosoc at the request of category A organizations have been: equal pay for equal work for men and women; trade union rights; forced labour; administration of oil resources.

NGO representatives regularly attend meetings of various United Nations organs and their active participation is of particular value to the technical committees of the regional economic commissions, and of course to the Specialized Agencies. They play an important part in support of the work of Unicef and the High Commissioner for Refugees.

Interested NGOs hold conferences on certain specific subjects dealt with by the United Nations. Migration is one of these problems, and several NGO conferences under the joint sponsorship of the United Nations and the International Labour Organisation have discussed how they could assist in bringing aid to migrants. Close co-operation has been established under United Nations suspices between the NGOs concerned with the prevention of crime and the treatment of offenders, and these bodies have held several conferences organized by the United Nations. Similar arrangements were made with NGOs interested in the rehabilitation of the physically handicapped.

The NGOs have established their own machinery to maintain close contact with the United Nations. They hold bi-annual general conferences of consultative NGOs, and these have done much to develop and to perfect the techniques of co-operation between the organizations and the United Nations. The NGO section of the Ecosoc secretariat acts as a general liaison office between the United Nations and the organizations. (The co-operation of the Specialized Agencies with the NGOs is described under separate headings.)

NGOS AND PUBLIC INFORMATION ABOUT THE UNITED NATIONS

Apart from the 300-odd NGOs which have consultative status with Ecosoc, thousands of international and national organizations are in close contact with the United Nations, through its Office of Public Information, and assist in spreading knowledge about the United Nations and its activities. This is in accordance with the basic policy of the United Nations to assist all organizations and to invite their co-operation in the dissemination of information.

The NGOs in fact perform on an ever-increasing scale the function of voluntary agents of the United Nations in the field of information. Through their large membership they are able to carry the story of the United Nations and its work to an ever wider general public. They reach the masses of the people everywhere. The NGOs are mainly responsible for the organization of United Nations Day and other international observances throughout the world.

At United Nations Headquarters and in the field through the network of United Nations Information Centres an everyday working contact is maintained with NGOs in more than eighty countries, who receive information material for further distribution, organize meetings and seminars, and who, in fact, represent public opinion as regards the United Nations.

The Office of Public Information maintains a list of about 270 representatives of national and international organizations at Headquarters. These representatives are invited to attend *ad hoc* briefings by officers of the General Assembly and senior members of the United Nations Secretariat and Specialized Agencies. They also receive information material issued by the United Nations family and have facilities to attend meetings at Headquarters.

In many countries national NGO committees have been formed with the express purpose of developing public understanding of the United Nations among their members and the general public. Study groups organized by NGOs frequently visit United Nations Headquarters and the Palais des Nations in Geneva, and seminars and courses are organized for these groups by United Nations information services.

On an international and a regional level, NGO conferences on public information are periodically held under the auspices of the Office of Public Information to enable the NGOs to express their views on current information problems, on projects for the execution of which their co-operation is invited, as well as on various aspects of the work of the United Nations.

Of particular value as regards information work done by the NGOs is the activity of the World Federation of United Nations Associations (WFUNA) and its numerous national associations all over the world. Nationally the United Nations Associations are both the centre and the moving spirit of NGO work for spreading knowledge about the United Nations. The international federation, closely co-operates with the Office of Public Information, organizing international seminars during sessions of the Assembly, of Ecosoc and of various Specialized Agencies.

BIBLIOGRAPHY

Material on the NGOs is rather scarce. The *Repertory of Practice of UN Organs,* Vol. III, article 71 (United Nations Publications, 1957) gives information on the execution of the provisions of the Charter concerning consultation with the NGOs. See also:

Articles in *Bulletin NGO-ONG,* Brussels.

Background paper on the OPI, April 1953. Document N 76.

International associations (former *NGO Bulletin-Bulletin ONG).*

Yearbook of international organizations, 1958-59. Seventh edition. Brussels, Union of International Organizations, 1958. 1269 pp.

Course XI

THE SPECIALIZED AGENCIES SYSTEM

INTRODUCTION

In fulfilment of the pledge of the United Nations Charter—'to employ international machinery for the promotion of the economic and social advancement of all peoples'—and of the objectives of Article 55 of the Charter, a remarkable expansion of international action and co-operation has taken place since the United Nations family of organizations came into being fifteen years ago. Their activities have made considerable progress towards achieving the ideal of universality; and this spread of their work throughout the world has been linked with almost complete universality as far as the membership of most of those organizations is concerned. New institutions affecting the welfare—and the very life—of millions of people have been created as organs of the United Nations or as Specialized Agencies, while other organizations, which were created before the United Nations came into being, have entered the system as Specialized Agencies.

In the course of the years, the methods and forms of international action, built largely on the basis laid down by the League of Nations, have undergone far-reaching changes. Organs of international action have become far more 'operational', their responsibilities extending to practical work in many fields in many countries, especially in the under-developed areas of the world. New methods have been developed, a noteworthy example being the world-wide exchange of 'know-how', and the sharing of skills, in the programme of technical assistance.

CO-OPERATION OF AUTONOMOUS INSTITUTIONS

The bulk of the work for raising the material and spiritual well-being of the world is done in the United Nations family by the Specialized

Agencies. They are autonomous bodies with their own policy-making and executive organs, their own secretariats and administration. The Charter, recognizing the desirability of decentralizing international economic and social action, nevertheless provided for close co-operation between the Agencies and the United Nations, and ensured this by prescribing that they be 'brought into relationship' with the United Nations.

The Economic and Social Council is the United Nations organ which co-ordinates the work of the Specialized Agencies on terms specified in an individual agreement made with each Agency which brings it into relationship with the United Nations. These agreements follow a standard pattern. They provide for reciprocal representation at meetings and the inclusion of items on the agenda when requested, exchange of information and documents, co-ordination as regards budgetary and financial arrangements, common technical and administrative services whenever possible and uniformity of personnel regulations. The Agencies agree, for their part, to take into consideration recommendations made to them by the United Nations and to report to the United Nations on the action taken by them to give effect to such recommendations.

The Agencies also agree to assist the Security Council in carrying out its decisions for the maintenance or restoration of international peace and security and to co-operate with the United Nations in its work for the welfare and development of dependent peoples.

THE AGENCIES

Agreements with the following 13 organizations are in force (in the chronological order of the signature of the agreements):
International Labour Organisation (ILO);
Food and Agriculture Organization (FAO);
United Nations Educational, Scientific and Cultural Organization (Unesco);
International Civil Aviation Organization (ICAO);
International Bank for Reconstruction and Development (BANK);
International Monetary Fund (FUND);
World Health Organization (WHO);
Universal Postal Union (UPU);
International Telecommunication Union (ITU);
World Meteorological Organization (WMO);
International Finance Corporation (IFC);
International Atomic Energy Agency (IAEA);[1]
Inter-governmental Maritime Consultative Organization (IMCO).

---

1. IAEA reports to the United Nations General Assembly and not to Ecosoc, as do the others.

CO-ORDINATION OF PROGRAMMES AND ACTIVITIES

Each year, at its summer session, Ecosoc makes a general review of the way in which the economic, social and human rights programmes and activities of the United Nations, and of the Specialized Agencies as a whole, are developing and being co-ordinated.[1] Ecosoc then deals with the economic development of underdeveloped countries; and the financing of this work; with the promotion of industrialization and productivity; with balanced development of industry and agriculture; with social aspects of industrial development; with conservation of natural resources; with the advancing of human rights and spiritual development. Broad programmes are mapped and formulated, and the Specialized Agencies are given responsibility for executing many important parts of these programmes.

Co-ordination at the working level in implementing the programmes is done by the Administrative Committee of Co-ordination (ACC) established by the Council to ensure the smooth functioning of the system of 'relationship'. It is composed of the Secretary General of the United Nations and the executive heads of the Specialized Agencies. The ACC is also the channel for consultation on administrative and budgetary matters, such as salary systems, financial regulations, common administrative services, and the common utilization and pooling of staff of various Agencies, particularly in the field of technical assistance.

Co-ordination and liaison in the field of public information is carried out through the Consultative Committee on Public Information set up under the ACC.[2]

In the preceding courses, certain activities of practically all the Agencies have been mentioned in connexion with the work of the United Nations itself and within the framework of co-ordinated action by the United Nations family. A description of the organization and activities of individual Agencies follows this present introduction. Once more it will be seen how far these activities are interconnected, and how much —particularly in technical assistance—the co-operation of the organizations forming the United Nations system has contributed to the well-being and progress of humanity.

---

1. See page 132 for bibliographical reference to *Appraisal of Unesco's programmes for the Economic and Social Council,* 1960.
2. For details see the course on public information on page 185.

PART II

UNITED NATIONS EDUCATIONAL, SCIENTIFIC AND CULTURAL ORGANIZATION (Unesco)

Of all the Specialized Agencies of the United Nations, Unesco is, in a sense, the least specialized. Its activities cover the immense and widely varied fields of education, science and culture throughout the world. It is heterogeneous by the very nature of its activities and by the diversity of needs of its Member States. In this it is unlike other agencies, which were given a specific, technically determined task, and which are faced in their work with more clearly defined and much less complex situations and problems.

ORIGIN AND ORGANIZATION

Unesco was born in time of war. In fact, it arose out of the second world war and out of the conviction that 'it is in the minds of men that the defences of peace must be constructed' (preamble to Unesco's constitution). Ministers of education of Allied Governments met regularly during the years 1942–45 in London to consider problems of education, in particular what post-war international action could be taken to rehabilitate the education system in occupied and war-devastated areas. Out of these conferences sprang the idea of extending the Institute of Intellectual Co-operation of the League of Nations into a wider international organization, the aim of which would be 'to contribute to peace and security by promoting collaboration among the nations through education, science and culture in order to further universal respect for justice, for the rule of law and for the human rights and fundamental freedoms . . .' (Article I of the Constitution).

A few months after the United Nations Conference in San Francisco, a conference in London attended by representatives of 44 countries adopted (on 16 November 1945) the constitution of the United Nations Educational, Scientific and Cultural Organization. The organization came into being on 4 November 1946. By November 1960 it had 98 members.

A General Conference consisting of delegates appointed by the governments of Member States meets every two years to review the organization's work, to select the Executive Board, to appoint the Director-General as necessary (he holds office for a term of six years), to admit new Member States, to determine policies and programmes, to vote the budget, to adopt conventions and recommendations for submission to Member States. The Executive Board of 24 members meets at least twice a year: it is responsible for preparing the agenda for the General Conference, for supervising the execution of the programme voted by the conference, and for recommending admission of new Member States. The secretariat consists of approximately 420 professional members plus office personnel numbering 575 persons, recruited from more than 55 Member States. In addition, some 80 persons are employed in field offices, plus technical assistance experts, about 400 of whom receive contracts annually for mission assignments.

The secretariat has been headed since December 1958 by Mr. Vittorino Veronese (Italy), Director-General, who succeeded Mr. Luther H. Evans (United States), 1953–58, Mr. John W. Taylor, acting Director-General 1952–53, Mr. Jaime Torres Bodet (Mexico), 1948–52, and Sir Julian Huxley (United Kingdom), 1946–48. The conference of 1958 adopted for the period 1959–60 a spending budget of $25,970,000 compared with $22,680,000 for the previous two years, 1957–58.

As provided for by the constitution, most member countries of Unesco have set up National Commissions, each consisting of representatives of the government and of national institutions and organizations interested in educational, scientific and cultural matters. The purpose of these commissions is to integrate individual efforts in Member States with the work of Unesco, to advise governments and delegations, to carry out liaison activities, and to function as outlets for information.

Some 400 NGOs (non-governmental organizations) co-operate with Unesco, 148 of them having consultative status. Direct subventions from Unesco are received by 40 of the organizations.

METHODS OF WORK: MAJOR PROJECTS

The priority fields of action for Unesco, laid down at the 1954 General Conference in Montevideo, are: expansion of free and compulsory education at the primary school level; development of 'fundamental education'—a term earlier used to describe not only literacy training, but also other basic education necessary for over-all community development and social and economic progress; reduction of racial, social and international tensions; fostering a more widespread mutual appreciation of Eastern and Western cultural values; sponsoring and assisting scientific research for the improvement of living conditions. At its 1954 session, the General Conference also authorized the preparation of proposals for 'major projects'; launched a special programme of aid called 'Participation in the Activities of Member States' and defined categories of 'general activities' and 'special activities' within Unesco's programme.

115

In 1956, the General Conference at New Delhi established three 'major projects' within the five above-mentioned priority fields of activity. They were: the extension of primary education in Latin America; scientific research for the development of arid lands; and mutual appreciation of Eastern and Western cultural values. (A 'major project' is one serving a large region, to be carried out, with augmented financial resources, over a period which may be as long as 10 years.)

It will be noted that Unesco's method of working is to concentrate on a number of major specific tasks for a given period, parallel with day-to-day activities. This concentration is imposed by the variety of Unesco's interests and tasks: in its early years when it was exploring all the diverse fields within its mandate, the organization was subjected to fairly widespread criticism that it was attempting too much and achieving too little. But now it has learned to marshal its resources and to concentrate its efforts with increasingly effective results. It is to some degree indicative of the growing interest won by Unesco's work that the organization's new headquarters building at Place de Fontenoy has become a leading Paris tourist attraction. Within a year of completion, Unesco House received its 100,000th paying visitor.

The organization of Unesco's secretariat reflects the main directions of its operations. It is divided into five programme departments: Education, Natural Sciences, Social Sciences, Cultural Activities, Mass Communication. There is also an Exchange of Persons Service, a Bureau of Relations with Member States, a Documents and Publications Service, and the usual administrative services.

EDUCATION

In spite of some improvements in the situation, half of the world's population remain unable to read or write, and there are still 200 million children of school age for whom no schools exist. In the field of education, therefore, Unesco's primary concern is both to fight illiteracy and to extend and improve school teaching. There is growing recognition by governments and international organizations that minimum standards of education are essential to any project of economic development, and many Member States are being helped in efforts to make free and compulsory education available to all their children. Expert advice is given on the building of schools and the training of teachers and on improvements of textbooks and of teaching materials. Special studies are conducted on problems which occur in school systems; missions are sent to help in dealing with various aspects of educational work; experimental projects and field operations are carried out.

It should be noted that Unesco's programme in education derives its unity from the concept, now prevalent in most countries, of permanent education—that is, of education as a continuing lifelong process extending from early childhood through adult life. But the intensity of the effort put into the various sectors of the programme naturally varies from time to time. For example, on the basis of the considerable momentum gained by the Major Project on the Extension of Primary Education in Latin America, the General Conference in 1958 gave the Director-General a mandate not only to conduct an inquiry into the educational needs of countries of tropical Africa, but also to survey the primary educational needs of Asia and the over-all educational outlook in Arab-speaking States. The findings and conclusions arrived at as a result of these inquiries have led to extensive developments in Unesco's education programme in Asia, Arab-speaking States and Africa.

Under the joint auspices of Unesco and the International Bureau of Education, world conferences to review problems of public education are held annually in Geneva. The 1959 conference was concerned, for instance, with the preparation, selection and use of textbooks for primary schools, and with the training of technical and scientific teaching staff.

Unesco also seeks to give every possible assistance to the improvement of technical and vocational education. This involves a number of ancillary studies and inquiries ranging from revision and modernization of the school curriculum to the contribution of sport to the improvement of professional abilities and cultural development (international conference held at Helsinki in August 1959).

An important example of Unesco aid to school programmes is the emergency assistance provided for Palestine Arab refugees. Established in 1949 under the administrative and financial responsibility of the United Nations Relief and Works Agency (UNRWA), this action provides primary education for more than 100,000 children in UNRWA/Unesco schools and for another 40,000 in government and private schools. Some 35,000 students are also receiving a general secondary education, 800 are benefiting from vocational training and about 400 are studying through awards of university scholarships. Unesco assumes technical responsibility for this broad programme and provides the higher directing staff, a number of internationally recruited experts who advise on the planning and execution of the programme as a whole and on the teaching of specific subjects.

In out-of-school education, the emphasis is placed on a programme for the general education of a community by giving adults and young people access to the knowledge necessary to understand the economic and social problems of their environment, including, if required, a minimum knowledge of health and hygiene, of community relations and of how to improve skill in agriculture and crafts. The principal features of this programme are therefore on the one hand to continue activities which will help Member States eradicate illiteracy, and on the other hand to assist adult and youth education projects, both of a governmental and non-governmental character. In connexion with the former objective, two regional centres to train leaders in this basic type of education have been set up and are receiving support from Unesco: 400 trainees from 19 countries have received training in the Latin American centre at CREFAL (Patzcuaro, Mexico) established in 1951, and 300 trainees from eight Arab States have completed their training at ASFEC (Sirs-el-Layyan, Egypt, United Arab Republic) established in 1953. The functions of these centres are being orientated increasingly towards community development.

As far as youth is concerned, the centre of current interest in the educational field is the social adaptation of young people. Action is carried out along two lines: social adaptation of youth and education of young people in international understanding and co-operation. General activities include help for about thirty international youth organizations and maintenance of contact with 'international relations clubs' in Member States, as well as with their voluntary work camps. Special youth subcommittees have been created by Unesco National Commissions in 25 countries. The purpose of these subcommittees is not only to inform young people about Unesco's work but also to support the activities of youth organizations which are educating their members in international understanding and preparing them to participate actively in the social and cultural life of their own communities. Groups of young people are encouraged to visit Unesco House in Paris to learn about its work at first hand. Seminars for youth leaders are organized at the Unesco Youth Institute in Gauting (Federal Republic of Germany) to study the methods and techniques of youth organizations and the problems related to the social maladjustment of young people. There is close co-operation between Unesco and the International Voluntary Work Camps Committee.

Besides encouraging the international exchange of correspondence between young people, Unesco takes a particular interest in facilitating travel abroad for educational purposes. Travel grants are available each year to some forty leaders of youth organizations. *Study Abroad*; *Vacations Abroad*; and *Travel Abroad: Frontier Formalities* are regularly published and contain valuable information for associations which organize study trips. Now in its eleventh edition, *Study Abroad* contains information on more than 90,000 individual study opportunities throughout the world. These periodical handbooks are published by the Exchange of Persons Service of Unesco.[1]

1. See page 130-131.

NATURAL SCIENCES

Unesco's contribution to scientific progress might be summed up as follows: it carries out the essential functions of bringing together scientists of different countries and of serving as a clearing house for the exchange of scientific knowledge both through personal contacts between scientists and through circulation of information.

The programme in the field of natural science may be divided into four main activities:

1. Promotion of international scientific co-operation, which covers the advancement of research in the basic sciences (mathematics, physics, chemistry, biology), exploratory studies on new scientific problems (such as those of nuclear physics, terrestrial space, information processing, electronic calculation, and cell biology), co-operation with scientific unions and councils, and the promotion of scientific documentation.
2. Promotion of studies and research relating to the natural resources of the earth's crust, the hydrosphere and the atmosphere.
3. Advancement of teaching and dissemination of science. This embraces activities relating to the advanced training of scientists and professors, missions to Member States by experts and professors, pemanent and travelling scientific exhibitions (13 of the latter have already been seen in 40 countries), the awarding of the annual Kalinga Prize for the popularization of science, and the development of associations for the advancement of science. (Twenty-seven countries were receiving technical assistance in 1959–60 to improve the teaching of science in their universities and schools.)
4. Regional activities, covering the activities (such as training courses, symposia, scientific meetings, and publications) carried out by four science co-operation offices which are maintained in Latin America, the Middle East, South Asia and South-East Asia.

A striking example of the role played by Unesco in stimulating and assisting the convening of meetings of specialists in various branches was afforded in June 1959, when the first International Conference on Information Processing was summoned at Unesco House and attended by some 2,000 specialists from 36 countries. This conference discussed the rapid development, the various implications and the uses of 'thinking machines' (such as electronic computation and mechanical translation of languages), and led to the creation of an international federation of information processing societies.

Another large conference, organized by the American Association for the Advancement of Science in collaboration with Unesco and the International Council of Scientific Unions, was the International Congress of Oceanography held at United Nations Headquarters in New York in

1959. About 1,200 specialists from 40 countries attended this congress, where the interest lay not only in the many fruitful exchanges between men of science but also in the realization that very little is yet known about the deep seas, their movements and resources. One direct outcome of this conference may be the establishment of an integrated system of oceanographic research by vessels and other means.

Through Unesco's initiative, what is now the autonomous European Organization for Nuclear Research (CERN) came into being in 1954 and built a central laboratory near Geneva, where fundamental research into the structure of matter is carried out by scientists from all over Europe. In this field of nuclear physics, important conferences were jointly organized by Unesco and the International Atomic Energy Agency (IAEA) in 1959. One, held at Saclay, near Paris, took up the problem of educating the specialists of the atomic age; the second, at Monaco, dealt with scientific aspects of the disposal of radio-active waste.

The arid lands major project is a highly important scientific undertaking on which Unesco is engaged, involving research and study on how to bring to life the desert or semi-desert areas which cover one-quarter of the globe's land surface. Guided by an advisory committee of distinguished scientists, specialists have been engaged since 1951 on studying how to use the vast reserves of underground water in arid areas, what to plant to protect fertile lands against encroachment by the desert, how vegetation and animal life are affected by arid zone climate, and how to use solar and wind energy in desert areas.

Recent research in this field led to a symposium on plant-water relationships which was held towards the end of 1959 in Madrid and attended by 52 specialists from 19 countries.

In addition, since 1956 Unesco has undertaken research projects into problems affecting the humid tropics.

As a result of a resolution of the United Nations General Assembly, Unesco was designated to act as the focal point of a survey on the main trends of inquiry in the field of the natural sciences and of the dissemination of such knowledge and its application for peaceful uses. Professor Pierre Auger (France), a former director of Unesco's Department of Natural Sciences, is in charge of this inquiry, and his report and recommendations were submitted to the Economic and Social Council in the summer of 1960.

SOCIAL SCIENCES

Unesco's programme of work in the social sciences is currently directed towards four main objectives. First, the maintenance and expansion of international professional associations and a documentation and clearing-house service. Second, the collection and analysis of statistics of education, science, culture and mass communication and the encouragement of better standardization of these statistics. Third, promotion of the development of social science teaching and research, especially in the less advanced countries, and dissemination of knowledge about research methods and the results achieved by research. Fourth, promotion of the more extensive and effective application of the social sciences to the study of selected social problems, in particular those related to social and economic development which interest the United Nations and the Specialized Agencies.

In the first years of Unesco's existence, almost all its work in the field of applied social sciences was devoted to undertaking and promoting studies on 'tensions affecting international understanding'. The first object of these studies was the production of a number of widely-differing publications—some general, such as the monographs in the *Way of Life* series, describing the political, social and cultural life of various countries in a manner calculated to encourage mutual understanding and to combat prejudice, and others more specialized, including volumes analysing the problems of tensions. In addition to this programme of publications, Unesco promoted original research on particular subjects, including the following: the attitudes of people in one country towards people of other countries; race prejudice and the roots of tension in local communities with different societies; the psychological causes of aggression.

Certain projects originally in a subordinate position in the programme proved very successful and were therefore developed. One of these was the study of demographic factors and especially of the integration of immigrants into a new cultural environment. Another was the question of tensions accompanying technological change. A third, which derived from a resolution of Ecosoc in 1950, dealt with the whole subject of racial discrimination. From these projects emerged the two topics which now dominate the programme of applied social sciences: (a) human rights; (b) the study of the social implications of industrialization and technological change. A further development, which was in part a by-product of this latter study, has been the improvement and application of techniques of evaluation, with special references to the evaluation of technical assistance and related activities.

There has been a rapid development of work on the social implications of industrialization and technological change. In this programme, particular importance has naturally been attached to those regions of the world where the most rapid changes are taking place, especially in Africa, South Asia and Latin America.

In the field of social sciences Unesco once again serves as a clearing house for basic documentation and reference; it publishes an *Interna-*

tional Social Science Journal, bibliographies on current publications in four series (economics, sociology, social and cultural anthropology, and political science) and various series giving the results of studies relating to the practical application of social science, and to the international problems mentioned in the second paragraph of this section.

In the series of studies on race relations, a major event in 1959 was the publication in the United Kingdom of Dr. Cyril Bibby's study, *Race Prejudice and Education*, aimed primarily at assisting teachers to overcome race prejudice in school. A German translation has also been published and a version in Hindi is in preparation.

Unesco also assists international organizations in calling meetings, an important recent example of international co-operation in the social sciences being the fourth World Congress of Sociology, held at Stresa, Italy, in September 1959. This brought together 800 participants from 40 countries who were able to take stock of the progress made in this direction over the past-century and discuss its application to problems arising in industry, agriculture, education, leisure and other aspects of modern life. As examples of other recent activity at a different level, mention may be made of field studies carried out on the social problems of industrialization and urbanization, as well as on the theory and practice of economic development, with relevant conferences being organized in various regions of the world. The status of the social sciences in Latin America is also a field of activity and Unesco is working in this regard with the Latin American Social Sciences Research Centre at Rio de Janeiro, Brazil, and the Latin American Social Sciences Faculty at Santiago de Chile. In both these centres, teacher training and research are carried out concurrently, while special courses and seminars bring social scientists throughout the continent together for shorter periods. Finally, the Department of Social Sciences operates the Unesco Research Centre on Social and Economic Development in Southern Asia, Delhi.

CULTURAL ACTIVITIES

As Unesco's resources are limited, it cannot aspire to take action throughout the infinite range of mankind's cultural riches, to which new treasures are continually being added, and which, incidentally, as a whole, are very often outside the competence of governmental or intergovernmental organizations. Its tasks are necessarily confined to carrying out or encouraging certain pilot projects, directing attention to cultural treasures which stand in danger or are not well enough known and, more particularly, to improving the necessary media for communication, comparison, collation and co-operation at the international level. These are the services which Unesco provides continuously in the broad fields of humanistic studies, arts and letters, copyright, monuments and museums, and libraries and archives—while concentrating as much as possible on problems of current urgency.

One such problem of special interest and compelling urgency came to the fore late in 1959, when Unesco took the initiative of organizing international action to safeguard the ancient Egyptian monuments in Nubia which are threatened with flooding by construction of the new Aswan Dam needed for industrial and agricultural developments. This action was organized at the request of the United Arab Republic and the Republic of Sudan, the two countries in which archaeological treasures are in danger. A plan of action was outlined and a world-wide appeal launched at the beginning of 1960, because the project of preserving these antiquities will ultimately involve large sums of money if certain of the temples, which cannot be moved, are to be effectively protected from the flood waters. An interesting feature of this project is the offer of both the UAR and the Sudanese governments to surrender a large proportion of the antiquities which can be saved and moved from the sites in Nubia. These would be handed over to such governments, archaeological units, etc., as might furnish aid, for permanent display in public museums in their own countries.

Another Unesco activity is the preparation and implementation of international conventions, such as the Universal Copyright Convention, which protects the interests of artists, writers and scientists. Thirty-four States were parties to this particular convention at the close of 1959. Under an agreement reached with the International Labour Organisation, Unesco and ILO are to collaborate in the preparation of an international instrument dealing with the protection of certain rights of performers, recorders and broadcasters which will eventually be submitted to an international conference. Thirty States are now parties to the Convention for the Protection of Cultural Property in the Event of Armed Conflict, and a beginning has been made with the registration of ancient monuments, etc., under the terms of this convention.

In the field of culture (as in other spheres of Unesco interest) the past few years have been marked by the continued growth of international contacts between specialists in various areas of learning and of the arts. Assistance is given to a wide variety of cultural projects such as libraries and museums, art education, restoration of monuments, archaeology, and so forth, each individual country being essentially responsible for taking the required action on its own account assisted by the grants made available for the purpose.

More than ten years' experience has clearly shown the importance of the work done and the results achieved, in collaboration with Unesco, by the international non-governmental organizations of scholars, writers, artists and others active in cultural life. For instance, in co-operation with the International Council of Museums (ICOM), which it helped to establish, Unesco produces *Museum*, an illustrated quarterly review which provides information on modern techniques of museum management, on the use of museums in school education and adult education, etc.

Much attention is devoted by Unesco to making better known the world's artistic treasures: travelling exhibitions of coloured reproductions bring the best art works of all ages to millions of peoples in all parts of the world; art albums devoted to lesser-known masters of painting are published in several languages; catalogues of coloured reproductions are issued, and, more recently, sets of coloured slides of the works of art illustrated in the albums have been made available at low cost.

In addition to its publications for library and museum specialists, Unesco organizes regional and international seminars to promote expansion and improvement of these public services.

Unesco has assisted in the setting up of three public library projects in India, Colombia and Nigeria as a spur to the establishment and growth of public library systems in those countries and surrounding regions.

Expert assistance is provided to help Member States in the establishment of libraries and museums and for the improvement of their various services and training of personnel.

In another field of activity, Unesco makes it possible for libraries to obtain works which were not accessible before. This is done by arranging for the publication of translations of representative works, either little known or requiring modern editions in English or French. These works have been drawn from more than twenty-eight literatures, including among others those of Latin America, Italy, Japan, China, India, Iran, Thailand and of various Arabic-speaking countries.

Unesco also compiles and publishes an annual catalogue of new translations published throughout the world. This comprehensive bibliography, now in its twelfth year, is called *Index Translationum*.

Through the International Theatre Institute (ITI) and its quarterly publication *World Theatre*, and through the International Music Council (CIM), international co-operation and exchange are facilitated in order to bring foreign plays to many countries, to make known contemporary music and folkmusic, and to encourage the performance of music and drama, especially among the young and in the schools. The role of the theatre and of music in education has been the subject of a number of interesting studies.

In many cultural fields, the organization of work at the international level was hitherto much less advanced than, say, in science, so Unesco has been instrumental in the establishment of several important new institutions. Examples are the International Council for Philosophy and

Humanistic Studies (ICPHS) which unites specialists in 13 different disciplines (this organization publishes, with Unesco assistance, a quarterly review, *Diogenes*, devoted to humanistic studies), and the International Association of Plastic Arts (IAPA). Other cultural organizations aided by Unesco include: the International Federation of Library Associations (IFLA); the International PEN Club; and the International Union of Architects (IUA).

In the field of arts and letters an essential element of Unesco's policy is to work through professional associations of artists, writers and crafts-men in their various spheres of activity. To this end, Unesco's work with representative groups is co-ordinated and planned with the help of a special liaison committee, which meets every two years.

THE EAST-WEST MAJOR PROJECT

References to two of the three major projects, adopted at the 1956 General Conference of Unesco, will be found under the headings of 'Education' and 'Natural Sciences'. It is more difficult to place under a specific heading the third Major Project for Mutual Appreciation of Eastern and Western Cultural Values. This is a project which taxes the resources of all the departments of Unesco and which requires the co-operation of research workers and experts in education, science and culture alike.

The aim of this project, which is to run for at least ten years, is to state clearly a problem of capital importance for the world today and to formulate methods by which Unesco can contribute to its solution. The project invites the co-operation not only of men of good will but also of Member States, of their National Commissions for Unesco, of their public and private institutions, of their media of information, and of non-governmental institutions which are actively associated with Unesco's work. Generally speaking, Western culture is considered, for the purposes of the project, as that prevailing in the European countries and other areas where the civilization is of European origin, while all non-European cultures, particularly those rooted in Asia, are regarded as Eastern. The task of defining more clearly the objective, the spirit and the methods of the project was entrusted to an international advisory committee. At its first session, in April 1957, this advisory committee unanimously stressed the importance of the project 'as a means of laying a sound foundation for lasting peace between nations . . . capable of dispelling the misunderstandings which all too often divide the peoples of the Orient and the Occident'. The committee has since held two more sessions: in February 1958 and in May 1959. In the light of its conclusions, how must the title of the major project be interpreted?

125

An answer to that question was given by Georges Fradier:[1] 'First, this title speaks of cultural values. These values are at the same time the highest creations of the human spirit and the more or less conscious ideals which are at work in the daily life of each people and give this life a truly human meaning. They are the traditions to which now-classical masterpieces have given expression, and they are also the ideas and the norms respected in modern societies in so far as these express the special genius of a nation and permit it to continue its development. "Cultural values", understood in this sense, are not the exclusive property of any one people or of any one culture; the resources of all are none too many for the spiritual equipment of the man of today.

'The word appreciation means more than mere knowledge. It introduces an element of sympathy, of warm adherence in which the foundation of a real moral solidarity can be discerned. On the other hand, it implies knowledge and understanding as its necessary conditions. Without real knowledge, without authentic understanding, appreciation is usually nothing more than a gratuitous fad.

'Finally, the appreciation of cultural values must be mutual. It is essential that every effort to make known the values proper to a culture be imbued with the spirit of reciprocity. This requirement gives the project a universal goal: to found on the dialogue among peoples the respect that they owe each other through the fact that they are engaged in the same adventure; while recognizing the absolute and irreplaceable value of each culture, to invite it to take its place in a common patrimony.

'True, the natural play of the instruments of cultural diffusion at present favours a current of exchanges running chiefly from West to East. A special effort is therefore needed, first of all, to spread among the general public in the West a more complete and more satisfactory knowledge of the cultural values of Asia and Africa. However, the major project also comprises activities to help the peoples of the East to obtain a more complete and more accurate image of Western civilization.'

Such is the spirit in which Unesco has undertaken this 10-year programme. Not all the details have been fixed; the lessons of experience necessarily lead Unesco to change the content considerably, to accept one or another aspect more or less, or to introduce new methods and activities.

The programme now being carried out by the organization in this field is divided into three principal parts. The first concerns studies and research which chiefly require the co-operation of specialists in the social sciences and humanistic studies; the second calls for action in the

---

1. In: *East and West: Towards Mutual Understanding,* Paris, Unesco, 1959, 49 pp.

teaching field; the third is directly aimed at the education of adults and the cultural life of the general public.

For the first stage of the project the target aimed at by Unesco was to ensure the participation of Member States in carrying out the programme, to organize international discussions by specialists and preliminary investigations of subjects to be treated, to improve school programmes concerning cultural values of the Orient and the Occident, and to stimulate exchange of information by using the modern media of mass communication, and by travelling exhibitions of reproductions of works of art. In the words of the Director-General (in his report on Unesco activities during 1959): 'Here an initiative taken by Unesco, or more exactly a principle laid down by Unesco, has, after due preparation, blossomed a thousandfold all over the world. . . . [In many ways] a great number of our Member States are actively promoting better understanding between the Orient and the Occident.'

MASS COMMUNICATION

Unesco's interest in the modern media of mass communication—press, film, radio, television—is twofold. At the inception of the organization it was recognized that a distinct programme area should be created with two basic functions, one of which is to promote the free flow of information and to help develop mass communication media and techniques. The other basic function is to enlist the assistance of the information media in making known the aims and activities of the organization and in furthering international understanding.

Public information on Unesco is organized very much as it is in the case of the United Nations and of the other Specialized Agencies: national media and outlets are supplied with written and illustrated material giving current information about the progress of Unesco's work; press material, films, filmstrips, kinescopes, radio recordings, photo stories and exhibitions are prepared and made available to assist in spreading accurate and objective information about the purposes and achievements of the organization and, when relevant, of other members of the United Nations family.

A monthly magazine, *The Unesco Courier*, published in English, French, Russian and Spanish contains articles of interest to the general public on a variety of subjects within Unesco's mandate. *Unesco Features*, a weekly news service, contains news items and articles related in general to international co-operation and understanding, and is designed primarily for newspapers which may be lacking adequate sources of world information of this sort.

In its work of 'advancing the mutual understanding of peoples through all means of mass communication' (Article I of the constitution),

Unesco works to facilitate the free flow of information; it promotes technical development of the mass media; and it seeks to bring about the fullest and most positive use of these media.

In order to reduce obstacles impeding the world-wide circulation of scientific, cultural and educational materials, Unesco sponsored an international agreement which eliminates customs duties on the importation of a wide range of articles such as books, works of art and scientific instruments. This agreement came into force in 1952, and by 1959 31 countries were applying it. In addition, the United States had signed the agreement and submitted it to the Senate for ratification. Another agreement, applied by 13 governments, covers films, sound recordings, maps, posters and other audio-visual material of an educational, scientific and cultural character, and exempts them from customs duties and import restrictions. Unesco also co-operates with the United Nations and other Specialized Agencies, such as ITU and UPU, in efforts to standardize and reduce rates for the dispatch of educational, scientific and cultural material as well for the sending of information.[1]

To overcome currency shortages and restrictions, which are a major obstacle to the exchange and purchase of books and other materials of a cultural nature, Unesco launched its international coupon scheme in 1948. Since then, countries with 'soft' currency have been able to buy coupons from Unesco and sell them to institutions or individuals who in turn use the coupons to pay for books, films or scientific material purchased in 'hard' currency countries. These coupons have gained immense popularity; since the start of the scheme, coupons to the value of $29 million have been issued by Unesco, which backs them with its own 'hard' currency reserve. Twenty-nine countries were applying this scheme in 1959.

A severe barrier to the free flow of information is the inadequacy of technical facilities—for example, printing equipment, news agencies, radio, television and film facilities—in many parts of the world. Unesco assists in overcoming these difficulties by supplying technical information to Member States and to professional groups, by promoting or carrying out studies on specific problems and making the results available to interested groups, and by sending experts to co-operate in improving and extending facilities. Between 1947 and 1951, surveys were made of press, radio and film facilities throughout the world and the results were reported in five volumes in Unesco's *Press, Film, Radio* series. A similar survey of television was made in 1952–54 and the results were published in *Television—A World Survey*.

These surveys have been the source of very valuable material for

---

1. For Unesco's co-operation with the United Nations on the question of freedom of information and human rights, see Course V, page 60.

persons engaged in information work anywhere. More important steps have, however, since been taken to bring Unesco's activity in this field up to date and to extend its scope greatly. As a consequence, the United Nations Economic and Social Council in 1959 sought Unesco's assistance for a series of new initiatives to promote freedom of information. The organization was requested to undertake a world-wide survey on the problems of helping underdeveloped countries to build up press, radio, film and television facilities. This survey is intended to enable the United Nations to evaluate what the countries need in the way of information media and of resources to carry out a programme of development. Unesco is conducting the survey by means of a series of regional meetings, the first of which was held in Bangkok in January 1960 to draw up a programme for South-East Asia. It will be followed by similar meetings for Latin America and Africa in 1961 and 1962.

The General Conference in 1956 included training for journalists as a sphere of activity in Unesco's mass communication programme. This step was taken on the recommendation of an international meeting of experts on professional training for journalism, held in April 1956, which stressed the importance of achieving the highest standards for the journalistic profession so that the press and other information media can play their part in strengthening public belief in freedom of information, as an essential element of democratic life and of the fundamental rights of man. The meeting recommended that regional or international centres be created in order to raise standards of journalism training: it urged a wider exchange of journalists and teachers of journalism between countries, the granting of advanced study facilities by universities to working journalists, and training fellowships for journalists in underdeveloped countries.

As an outcome of this, an International Centre for Higher Education in Journalism was opened at the University of Strasbourg in October 1957, to serve countries in Europe, North Africa and the Middle East. Towards the end of 1959, Unesco assisted in the creation of an International Centre for Higher Studies in Journalism in Latin America parallel to the one in Strasbourg, at the Central University of Ecuador, in Quito, following recommendations from an expert meeting in that city convened by Unesco in 1958. Similar measures for promoting better journalism training in Asia and Africa were then being planned.

In recent years it has been possible for the Mass Communication Department of Unesco to extend its interests and activities through co-operation with a number of specialized international organizations which have come into being, some of them through Unesco's initiative. Examples of the latter are: the International Centre of Films for Children (Brussels), the International Association for Mass Communication Research (Paris), and the International Film and Television Council

(Rome). These non-governmental organizations carry out additional functions of information, research and co-ordination within their specialized spheres.

EXCHANGE OF PERSONS

One of the most rewarding of Unesco's enterprises is the promotion of study abroad. This is, indeed, an essential element in Unesco's work to develop greater international understanding and a more effective sharing of knowledge and skills among Member States. In practical terms the implementation of this design means, in most cases, helping people to overcome obstacles which bar free access to sources of knowledge in foreign countries: costs of travel, the required currency, passports, visas, lodging problems, language difficulties, and so on.

It is Unesco's policy in this regard that opportunities for study and training abroad should not only be available to those having access to specialized educational facilities, but should also be extended to include workers and young people and many other groups of men and women who wish to benefit from direct contact with persons from other lands and thereby improve possibilities of international understanding.

The clearing house of the Exchange of Persons Service provides both a focal point and a reliable source for information about the facilities offering for travel and study abroad. It collects and disseminates information on international fellowships and scholarships, and on enrolment by foreign students at teaching institutions, on opportunities for vacation study, on teaching posts which are offered abroad, on organizations which assist international travel. This and related information is available in the publications of the service, which include the periodical handbooks already referred to earlier in this section:[1] *Study Abroad: International Handbook of Fellowships, Scholarships and Educational Exchange*; *Vacations Abroad: Courses, Study Tours, Work Camps*; and *Travel Abroad: Frontier Formalities*.

The Exchange of Persons programme now covers extensive movements of groups of workers in Europe, the Americas and Asia, and of youth groups during the summer months.

The programme of fellowships, study and travel grants, etc., operates on the basis of a small nucleus of fellowships and grants financed directly out of Unesco's budget and a very much larger number of 'Unesco-sponsored' fellowships paid for by governments, foundations and other bodies and placed by them under Unesco's auspices. Special fellowship and study grant programmes are run in connexion with the major

---

1. See page 118.

projects. Much experience has been acquired in, and care given to, the selection of candidates, the formulation of their programmes of study, and the maintenance of contact with fellows after they have completed their studies. This last point is of particular importance under the technical assistance and participation programmes,[1] under which fellowships for study abroad are almost invariably given to the local 'counterparts' whose role it is to take over the direction of projects after the departure of the international expert who has set the project in motion.

Unesco Travel Coupons facilitate travel abroad for educational and cultural purposes for people from countries with exchange restrictions.

RELATIONS WITH MEMBER STATES

Relations with Member States are entrusted to a bureau which attends to the political, diplomatic and formal aspects of such of the Unesco secretariat's correspondence and activities as are of direct concern to governments and National Commissions.

Procedures for negotiations with Member States in connexion with preparing and implementing the participation and technical assistance programmes, and the programme of the Special Fund, come within the purview of the bureau. Another of its tasks is co-operation with the central United Nations organs which are responsible for the over-all administration of technical assistance and the Special Fund. It also keeps in constant touch with the resident representative of the Technical Assistance Board in various parts of the world and with Unesco experts on mission. Special attention is paid to securing a balanced geographical distribution of the organization's activities by region and by country, as well as a harmonious development of the various programmes within a particular country or a particular region.

Under technical assistance and its own programme of participation in the activities of Member States, Unesco had 255 experts on mission assignments in more than fifty-five countries by the end of 1959. Beginning in Afghanistan, Unesco experts could be found teaching mechanical technology or, at the other end of the alphabet, in Viet-Nam, working in rural community development campaigns. In between, other examples of their tasks included maintaining precision instruments in Burma, training teachers in Ethiopia, teaching engineering in India, and applying geophysics to the problems of arid lands in Pakistan.

These are only a few examples of what Unesco is doing under the United Nations Expanded Programme of Technical Assistance and its own programmes for participation in activities of Member States. Indeed, it might well be said that most of the activities of the organization fall

---

1. See page 81.

under the general heading of technical aid, so much direct and indirect help is now being given, and so many services rendered, to the governments and to the public in the Member States of Unesco in their efforts to attain higher levels of education, science and culture. And if this generalization is valid now it is likely to be even more so in the future. For an innovation of very great importance in this connexion was the start in 1959 of operations of the United Nations Special Fund, as a result of which Unesco rapidly found itself assigned responsibility for a number of Special Fund projects, the total cost of which, at the close of the year, was in the neighbourhood of $7 million. These projects included two technological institutes in India, a polytechnic school in Iran, a higher technical institute in Libya, an engineering school in the University College of the West Indies, and the development of the Middle East Technological University located at Ankara (Turkey). In view of the magnitude of the operations involved, as compared with the 'pilot project' size of most technical assistance and participation projects, it is clear that this new Special Fund programme has placed very large additional responsibilities upon Unesco.

REFERENCE AND BIBLIOGRAPHY

SPECIALIZED AGENCIES

In general the books on the United Nations and on international organizations listed in the bibliography for Course I also contain material on Specialized Agencies. One should add:
CHEEVER, D. S.; HAVILAND, H. F. *Organizing for peace. International organization in world affairs.* Boston, Houghton Mifflin, 1954.

UNESCO

Appraisal of Unesco's programmes for the Economic and Social Council. Paris, Unesco 1960. 182 pp. In accordance with the decision of Ecosoc in July 1957, concerning the appraisal of the programmes of the United Nations and the Specialized Agencies, this study was produced by Unesco to provide: '(a) an appraisal of its main programmes, as reviewed in 1959; (b) a forecast of the scope, trend and cost of these programmes for the years 1960-64'. It covers the following areas of work:
  1. Development of National Commissions.
  2. Development of international co-operation among specialists.
  3. Improvement of documentation.
  4. Development of school and higher education.
  5. Development of out-of-school education.
  6. Aid to research in the various branches of science.
  7. Application of the social sciences to social problems.

8. Preservation of the cultural heritage of mankind.
9. Mutual appreciation of cultural values.
10. Free flow of information and improvement of information media.
11. International training of specialists.
12. Implementation of human rights.

For each of these 12 areas of work, the study comprises three sections on the following pattern: the problem (needs to be met; possibilities of action and aims of the organization); retrospective study (efforts made and methods used; costs incurred up to 1959; assessment of results); future prospects (future programmes; budgetary implications).

Unesco Chronicle. A monthly report from Unesco House. Information on current activities of Unesco, on action in the field and special articles on projects.

Unesco in brief. Second edition. Paris, Unesco, 1959. A condensed outline of Unesco's work and results.

Unesco—ten years of service to peace. Paris, Unesco, 1956. A popular pamphlet.

What is Unesco? Second edition. Paris, Unesco, 1960. *(Unesco information manual,* No. 1.) A detailed, well organized guide to Unesco's activities.

Yearbook of the United Nations. Contains in each annual edition a chapter on Unesco.

BESTERMAN, Theodore. *Unesco, peace in the minds of men.* London, Methuen, 1951. 132 pp. Although published in 1951, this still is a standard book on Unesco.

LAVES, Walter H. C.; THOMSON, Charles A. *Unesco: purpose, progress, prospects.* Bloomington, Indiana University Press, 1957. 465 pp.

Various publications have been mentioned in the text of this course. Catalogues can be consulted in specialized bookshops and at national distributors of Unesco publications in many countries, the list of whom is given in most of the publications.

Course XII

SPECIALIZED AGENCIES: SOCIAL AND HUMANITARIAN

INTERNATIONAL LABOUR ORGANISATION (ILO)

The International Labour Organisation was brought into relationship with the United Nations in December 1946—it was thus the first of the United Nations Specialized Agencies. It has, indeed, established the precedent of the relationship between an intergovernmental institution, entrusted with specific tasks, and a universal international organization. In the belief that peace can only be based on social justice, ILO was established in 1919 as an autonomous institution, associated with the League of Nations: its constitution formed part of the Treaty of Versailles.

ILO has more than forty years of work behind it in a world which has been changing rapidly and which has gone through a second world war. The organization has been changing, too, adjusting itself and adapting its policies and machinery to new conditions. During the war, the organization transferred its working centre from Geneva to Montreal and went on making plans for its post-war activities. In 1944 the International Labour Conference met in Philadelphia and adopted a Declaration, which was annexed to its constitution. This Declaration reaffirmed the basic principles of ILO: that labour is not a commodity, that freedom of expression and of association are essential to progress, that poverty anywhere constitutes a danger to prosperity everywhere, and that the war against want requires to be carried on within each nation as well as by concerted international action. The Declaration included among its objectives full employment, the raising of living standards, extension of social security and welfare legislation.

The increased membership of the organization, together with the fact that many of the new members are countries from Asia, Africa, and the Middle East, which have newly become independent and are situated in what is known as the underdeveloped areas of the world, has also had a marked effect on the work of ILO. The activities of the organization have spread beyond the sphere of labour relations in industrialized countries to problems of social conditions in countries struggling for economic development, to the effects of industrialization, to questions of agriculture, handicraft and the co-operative movement. The methods of work have also undergone an evolution. The organization has embarked upon operational activities in different regions of the world.

'We are living', said the Director-General of ILO, David Morse, in a recent article in the *Annals of the American Academy of Political and Social Science*, 'through a social transition of tremendous importance to the future of mankind. It is a transition towards industrialization and independence in an increasingly interdependent world community. . . . Our essential problem is . . . to learn how to combine economic progress with social progress, to combine the search for improved social well-being with the search for greater human freedom. The heart of the probelm lies in the field of social organization and social relationship. ILO, which deals with labour and social policy in a wide sense, should accordingly be able to make a unique contribution to peace and orderly change throughout the world.'

HOW ILO IS ORGANIZED

The three organs of ILO are: the Internatonal Labour Conference; the Governing Body; and the International Labour Office.

The conference, the policy-making body, meets annually. Each member country sends a delegation of four: two government representatives, one employer delegate, and one worker delegate. Each delegate has one vote in the conference.

The conference's principal function is to establish international social standards in the form of international labour conventions and recommendations. The conference elects members of the Governing Body, and adopts the budget. It provides a forum for discussion of problems of social policy which are of concern to all countries. This is done in the course of the 'general debate', based on the annual report of the Director-General, who selects topics of pressing international importance to be the central theme of the year. The 1959 report detailed the activities of the organization during the year and discussed current problems and trends. More than 900 delegates, advisers and observers attended the 1959 conference.

The Governing Body is the executive organ of ILO. It is composed of 40 members: 20 representatives of governments, 10 of the employers, and 10 of the workers. Each of the three groups elects its own representatives, except for the government representatives from the countries holding permanent seats as States of prime industrial importance: Canada, China, France, Federal Republic of Germany, India, Italy, Japan, the United Kingdom, the United States and the USSR. Elections take place every three years.

The International Office, located in Geneva, is the permanent secretariat of ILO, headed by the Director-General, who is elected by the Governing Body. Mr. David A. Morse, of the United States, is the Director-General.

The office has branches at Bonn, London, New Delhi, Ottawa, Paris, Rio de Janeiro, Rome, Tokyo, and Washington, and national correspondents in many countries. (Moscow, Buenos Aires and Cairo were added in 1959.)

Membership of ILO on 21 November 1960 was 95. Its draft budget for 1961 is $10.2 million.

TRIPARTITE STRUCTURE

The most distinctive feature of ILO is its tripartite structure: the fact that government representatives, employers, and workers participate side by side directly in its annual conference, in the Governing Body and other organs, with an equal right to vote. The employers' and workers' delegates are not bound to follow governmental instructions. They may, and often do, disagree with their government's policy and with each other.

The employers' and workers' delegates meet separately whenever they deem it necessary, to discuss among themselves questions on the agenda of meetings.

THE INTERNATIONAL LABOUR CODE

The work of ILO is done by setting international labour and social standards; by providing technical assistance and expert advice to its members in their efforts to improve social conditions; by research work done by the office; by gathering and distributing information on problems with which the organization is dealing.

The 114 conventions and 112 recommendations adopted since the creation of ILO now form an imposing International Code of Labour, setting standards which cover: general conditions of employment, hours of work, minimum wages, paid holidays, protection of seamen; conditions of employment of women and young people, equal pay for women, night work, maternity protection, minimum age, medical examination, and protection of young persons; social security, freedom of association, trade union rights, forced labour and migration.

The conventions and recommendations are adopted by a two-thirds majority. Conventions enter into force when a sufficient number of Member States ratify them. Recommendations are not subject to ratification. If a convention is ratified, the government must report on the measures taken to give effect to it.

The conventions are the result of long and patient work, of much research and detailed debate. In most cases they are based on the experience of Member States, and reflect the progress already achieved by them. The preliminary work, accompanied by discussion and comment from interested groups in the member countries, not only creates a favourable atmosphere for subsequent adoption and ratification, but often leads also to measures by the governments which anticipate the provisions of a Convention.

The ILO Conference examines each year a report on the extent to which member countries fulfil their obligations in respect of international labour standards. This report is presented by a group of experts and jurists who study the information furnished by the governments.

The present number of ratifications is nearly 2,000. Ninety-four conventions have received a sufficient number of ratifications to come into force.

The number of ratifications has doubled in the past ten years; the new members ratify many conventions immediately on entering the organization and, generally, members are speeding up their ratification procedures.

A notable change has occurred in the type of problems which have become the subjects of conventions. Initially, ILO was preoccupied with the need to regulate conditions of work and to assure social protection; not least, to do away with abuses that had revealed themselves in industrialized societies. The next stage was marked by wider social planning, to avoid the abuses of the earlier processes of industrialization and to spread the benefits of economic development to all classes of society. After the second world war the emphasis shifted to full employment and higher living standards, to fundamental issues of freedom of association and the right to organize, to the great problems of industrial development in the less developed countries, to studies on social conditions of industrialization, the movements of workers from rural to urban areas, labour relations in agriculture and handicraft.

TECHNICAL SERVICES AND TECHNICAL ASSISTANCE

Reshaping its machinery and its activities in response to the needs and conditions of post-war years, ILO has been laying more stress on its advisory services and operational work, particularly since the United Nations Expanded Programme of Technical Assistance has opened possibilities which had never existed before.

True, since its beginning in 1919, ILO had been offering technical services known as 'advisory missions' to its members. Teams of experts were visiting countries to assist in implementing conventions or to give advice on labour problems. Member governments have also relied on ILO services for information on various social questions. However, the picture changed radically after the second world war. Increasing emphasis had to be placed on providing assistance to the efforts of governments to raise standards of living and productivity, and on passing on the skills and experience of the more advanced industrialized countries to the less developed regions of the world.

The funds of the Expanded Programme enabled ILO to undertake these 'operational' activities on a larger scale than ever before. For the year 1959 the funds expended by ILO under the Expanded Programme totalled approximately $3,270,000. The ILO share in the technical assistance funds is about 11 per cent and, in recent years, 60 countries and territories have received assistance annually.

About half the assistance is concerned with the use of manpower, in particular with the improvement of vocational training. About a quarter has been related to labour conditions and administration. The remainder has been devoted to productivity centres and missions, the co-operative movement, handicrafts and social security. Three hundred and three ILO experts were on assignments and 207 fellowships were granted in 1959, including worker-trainee awards for study and work in factories abroad or in regional training institutes.

Training in the centres, established with the assistance of ILO and organized in such a way as to be run later by the countries concerned, is of great variety; for example, maintenance of motor vehicles in Indonesia, of bulldozers in Pakistan, of diesel engines for water transport in Burma, productivity and vocational training in India, Turkey, Ecuador, Haiti, Libya, management training in Yugoslavia, and so on.

ILO bears the over-all responsibility for the regional Andean Indian project aimed at raising the standard of living of the indigenous populations of Bolivia, Peru, and Ecuador, in which FAO, WHO and Unesco also participate.

Other examples of ILO's co-operation with other Agencies are: ILO furnished handicraft training instructors for various Unesco fundamental education centres; FAO experts joined ILO missions in the field of agricultural co-operation.

INDUSTRIAL COMMITTEES

Another significant post-war extension of ILO activities was the creation of industrial committees in 1946, to deal more effectively with particular problems of individual industries. The committees have a tripartite membership and have been set up for eight industries (building, chemicals, coal-mining, inland transport, iron and steel, metal trades, petroleum, textiles) and salaried employees and professional workers.

Since the early days of ILO a Joint Maritime Commission and a Special Maritime Section of the conference have been instrumental in initiating many reforms in the conditions of seafarers. There is also an Asian Advisory Committee and an African Advisory Committee. The latter had its first session in Luanda (Angola) in December 1959. Apart from these committees, ILO has panels of consultants for occupational safety and health, women's work, juvenile employment, labour statistics and co-operation, indigenous labour and recreation (including workers' education).

STUDY OF SPECIAL PROBLEMS

In 1958 the Governing Body decided to make a survey of conditions relating to freedom of association, especially the freedom of the trade union movement. A study group has visited the United States and the USSR. Other member countries have also invited ILO to make surveys.

The organization is now also engaged on a world-wide study of the progress of workers' education, of training of management personnel, and of training of social service administration.

The growing use of atomic energy in industry raises many problems of concern to ILO, such as the protection of workers against radiation, and the need for special training, etc. Eight experts have established model regulations for the protection of workers against radiation. On the creation of the International Atomic Agency, ILO established close co-operation with the new organization.

Another question which has exercised ILO is that of automation and the effects it will have on workers. Recent activity in this field included a meeting in Cologne (at the invitation of the Federal Republic of Germany) in December 1959, of the ILO Advisory Committee on Salaried Employees and Professional Workers which gave detailed attention to the effects of automation on office workers.

Publications of ILO cover a wide field of social problems. The monthly *International Labour Review* contains articles on economic and social topics, statistics on employment, wages, consumers' prices. The fortnightly *Industry and Labour* gives information on activities of ILO and on current events in industrial relations, employment, migration, the activities of workers' and employers' organizations. The *Legislative Series*, a compilation of industrial legislation, the *Yearbook of Labour Statistics, Occupational Safety and Health* are other regular ILO publications. Studies and reports are published on economic and social subjects, on technical problems, on legislation and administrative practice.

The *ILO News*, a periodical in several languages, is destined for the use of public information media. The ILO public information service also issues pamphlets on ILO activities and press releases on current events; it provides radio material and produces documentary films. Information material on ILO can be had directly from headquarters at Geneva, from branch offices and from United Nations information centres.

REFERENCE AND DOCUMENTATION

Concerning the activities of ILO, 1959-60, see: *Report of the Director-General to the forty-fourth session of the International Labour Conference*. Geneva, ILO, 1960. See also previous annual reports.

The International Labour Organisation since the war. Geneva, ILO, 1953.

The International Labour Code. A systematic arrangement of the conventions and recommendations with appendixes and notes. Geneva, ILO, 1954. Two volumes.

A number of brochures on the various aspects of the work of the organization is available from the Information Service of ILO, e.g.:

Safety and health of workers.
The ILO and women.
Youth at work.
Partner for progress: ILO's technical assistance programme.
The ILO's workers' education programme.
ILO's 40th anniversary, 1919-59.

WORLD HEALTH ORGANIZATION (WHO)

International action in the field of health and hygiene grew organically with social and industrial progress, as it did in other spheres of human activity. The fact that the world was rapidly growing smaller, that diseases and epidemics had begun to follow the fast trade and travel routes led to the first attempt at international co-operation in public health more than 100 years ago—the calling of a 12-nation conference in 1851 which tried to achieve uniformity of quarantine regulations in ports to prevent the spread of pestilence.

Other international meetings followed and gradual progress was made until, in 1902, the Pan-American Sanitary Bureau, and, in 1907 the Office International d'Hygiène Publique in Paris, were created to watch for and to report the outbreak of diseases, and to ensure effective application of international sanitary conventions that had been signed in the meantime.

Co-operation in public health was extended with the establishment of the League of Nations. Its Health Organization concerned itself not only with major disease problems, but also with studies on nutrition, housing and standardization of therapeutic substances. During the second world war it was decided that health work would be one of the primary and fundamental responsibilities of UNRRA, thus providing the indispensable link between continuing intergovernmental health activities before and after the war. The road was paved for WHO. At the San Francisco Conference of 1945, health was included in the United Nations Charter as one of the essentials of peace and well-being. The constitution of WHO was adopted the following year at an international conference in New York, and on 1 September 1948, the organization was established as a Specialized Agency of the United Nations, with headquarters in Geneva, at the Palais des Nations.

ORGANIZATION

The World Health Assembly referred to above is the highest authority of WHO. It meets every year to determine policies and programmes, and to vote the annual budget. Its Executive Board, which meets twice a year, is a technical non-political body, composed of 18 health experts, designated by as many Member States elected by the Assembly, but not representing their governments.

Expert committees composed of specialists from all parts of the world advise the organization on various technical aspects of health.

The activities of WHO are decentralized. Six regional offices have been created; in New Delhi for South-East Asia; in Alexandria for the Eastern Mediterranean; in Manila for the Western Pacific; in Washington, where the Pan-American Sanitary Bureau acts as the regional office for the Americas; in Brazzaville, French Equatorial Africa, for Africa south of the Sahara; and in Copenhagen, for Europe. Regional committees, consisting of representatives of Member States in the region, meet once a year, supervise the work of regional offices and work out regional programmes.

A secretariat of about 1,000 international officers from 63 countries, at headquarters in Geneva and at the regional offices, is headed by the Director-General, Dr. M. G. Candau, of Brazil.

The annuel budget for 1959 amounted to $15 million. In addition WHO participates to the extent of about $5 million a year in the Expanded Programme of Technical Assistance.

Every year 7 April is celebrated by member countries as World Health Day.

METHODS OF WORK

According to its constitution, WHO is the 'directing and co-ordinating authority on international health work' and as such it is at the disposal of national health administrations to help improve their health services. It is not primarily concerned with the treatment of diseases, but rather with prevention, and the improvement of sanitary conditions, nutrition standards and health services, and with promoting the physical, mental and social well-being of the peoples of the world.

THE CAMPAIGN AGAINST MALARIA

The world-wide malaria campaign is one of the main concerns of WHO at the present time. It is the greatest international health programme ever undertaken and the first programme to aim at the universal eradication of a disease. The malaria eradication campaign was launched in 1955, following a resolution of the eighth World Health Assembly. It has already achieved remarkable results and consolidated work previously done, as shown by the following facts.

The trend of malaria incidence, reported from countries totalling between a quarter and a third of the world's population, shows that the figure of about 250 million malaria cases that occurred annually until 1950 had been reduced by 30 per cent at the end of 1955, and by a further 20 per cent by the end of 1957.

In the same period deaths from the disease fell from 2.5 million a year to 1 million, according to the most recent estimates.

At present, out of a total world population of 2,800 million, about 1,408 million live in zones that are actually or potentially malarious. Some 279 million had been freed from the threat of malaria by the end of 1959. Another 684 million live in the 62 countries and territories where malaria eradication is now in progress, and 167 million live in 16 countries and territories in which malaria eradication programmes are in the planning stage.

A race is now under way between the deadly properties of insecticides and the growing resistance shown by the mosquitoes. World-wide research is being done and WHO malaria teams are assisting in carrying out local tests of mosquito susceptibility to different insecticides. A survey has been made of the current state of research on theses question. WHO consultants visited more than 100 laboratories concerned with resistance problems. A committee of experts on insecticides studied their reports, determined the gaps in existing knowledge and drew up a plan for developing methods of measuring the susceptibility or resistance of insects to insecticides. An extensive system has been established for exchange of information on problems of resistance in general, involving 300 workers in the field.

To meet the requirements of individual countries carrying out malaria eradication campaigns, the World Health Organization set up the Malaria Eradication Special Account for voluntary contributions from governments and private sources. In May 1960, about $12 million had been received, by far the largest part from the United States, this sum being more than $7 million short of the amount needed to continue to carry out WHO's share of the expenses of eradication until the end of 1961.

ADVISORY SERVICES

WHO is helping governments to combat many diseases besides malaria, by furnishing expert consultants and by sending demonstration teams of specialists to help to develop modern techniques of fighting and controlling disease and to train personnel. Tuberculosis, although rapidly declining, still ranks among the world's greatest killers. The risk of its spread is diminished by the large-scale BCG vaccination campaigns assisted by WHO and Unicef which have already reached 200 million people in 58 countries. Tuberculosis is a universal problem, and its eradication is not yet possible except perhaps in a few highly developed countries. In less advanced areas where there are not enough hospitals, WHO is now helping to perfect large-scale methods using inexpensive drugs such as isoniazid to treat patients at home.

Yaws, a crippling infection, threatens half the population of tropical areas. One hundred million people have already been examined and 25 million given penicillin injections in mass campaigns assisted by WHO and Unicef. The cost is only 10 or 15 cents per person treated.

Among preventable diseases that cause widespread suffering and dire economic loss to the world are leprosy, trachoma (an eye infection), venereal diseases, rabies, brucellosis (undulant fever), bilharziasis (snail fever) and other parasitic diseases, dysenteries, smallpox, yellow fever, cholera and typhus. WHO assists national efforts to prevent or control these and many others.

All these diseases mainly affect the underdeveloped parts of the world, where WHO's assistance and advice are particularly needed. The organization also pays great attention to diseases prevalent in the economically advanced countries—influenza and poliomyelitis, for instance. The World Influenza Centre in London directs a network of laboratories in 45 countries and important studies have been published on polio and the new vaccines, the result of co-ordinated research by laboratories throughout the world. WHO is now planning an extensive research programme in the field of cancer and heart disease.

PUBLIC HEALTH SERVICES

Lack of properly trained health personnel is probably the most serious brake on health progress throughout the world. WHO has accordingly devoted considerable efforts to education and training. Through its fellowship programme, advanced study abroad has already been made available to more than 10,000 qualified health workers—doctors, nurses, sanitary engineers, midwives, statisticians and others. Together with Unicef, WHO is engaged in training personnel for maternal and child health and welfare centres. The organization aims at making mental health an integral part of public health programmes, and particular attention is being paid to alcoholism. WHO is working with FAO on nutrition problems in relation to infant diseases and particularly parasitic infections. Sanitation forms a part of nearly every WHO programme; problems of waste disposal, of pure water supply, of pure food, and destruction of insects and vermin. In close collaboration with ILO, WHO deals with problems of industrial hygiene, medical aspects of social security, health services for seamen, and rehabilitation of the physically handicapped.

TECHNICAL SERVICES

The organization also carries out a number of services that it inherited from former health organizations. The five great pestilences of history—plague, cholera, smallpox, typhus and yellow fever—still linger on, an ever-present menace in our age of rapid air and sea transport. WHO maintains a watchdog service that collects and broadcasts precise information daily by short-wave radio to health authorities, ports, airports, and ships at sea. WHO is also able to pass on to national health services information concerning outbreaks of virus diseases such as influenza and poliomyelitis, obtained through its world network of scientific centres.

Until recently, little uniformity existed in quarantine regulations and excessive measures at some frontiers resulted in costly delays to travel and trade. In 1952, WHO's Member States adopted a uniform set of International Sanitary Regulations which give maximum protection against the spread of disease while avoiding undue interference in land, sea and air traffic.

WHO recommends international standards of strength and purity of medical products and has published several volumes of *International Pharmacopoeia* with many hundreds of prescriptions and specifications for use in all countries. It co-operates with the United Nations in the international control of narcotics.

Medical research is encouraged and supported all over the world.

WHO helps to establish laboratories, co-ordinates the work of research centres on virus and communicable diseases, and promotes demonstrations of new methods for preventing and curing these diseases. For complex biological substances such as vaccines, antibiotics, hormones and others, WHO has adopted international standard preparations which are held by laboratories in London and Copenhagen and made available to laboratories throughout the world for purposes of comparison with other preparations. This work was started by the League of Nations which adopted a standard preparation for diphtheria anti-toxin. Today the number of substances for which there are international biological standards exceeds a hundred.

ATOMIC ENERGY AND PUBLIC HEALTH

The growth of the peaceful uses of atomic energy means that more people are exposed to the effects of radiation. Present and future generations must be safeguarded against this new health hazard, and WHO is called upon to share this responsibility with the United Nations and other international bodies. Radio-active wastes, if not carefully disposed of, may dangerously pollute the air, soil and water, and increased background radiation may even have harmful effects on the heredity of the human race. WHO is required to help national health administrations to train the large numbers of health personnel needed in this field, and to collect and disseminate information and promote research which will provide the basis for action to hold the levels of radiation, from all sources, within internationally accepted limits. Another subject on which WHO is required to keep its members informed is that of radio-isotopes which are being used more and more widely for medical and research purposes.

WHO participates in the work of the United Nations on the effects of atomic radiation: it collaborates with ILO on protection of workers against radiation in industry, with FAO on sterilization of food by radiation, with Unesco on regulations for the transport of isotopes and on the effects of radiation on animal genetics.

RESEARCH

Types of research which can best be carried out through international co-operation have taken a prominent place in WHO's activities. WHO is undertaking world-wide studies on cancer and heart diseases, and on communicable diseases such as tuberculosis and influenza. Assistance is given to countries which lack adequate research resources.

The public information division issues regular press releases on the activities of the organization and on conferences and meetings of its organs. It also has a feature service on health subjects and publishes a magazine, *World Health*, mainly for the use of the press, radio and other media, in several languages. In co-operation with United Nations radio, it broadcasts frequently in English, French, Portuguese, Russian and Spanish. It has produced several documentary films and it carries out a regular distribution of still photos. Plentiful material for all information media is available for World Health Day. Seminars and courses on the work of WHO and on public health problems are held at Geneva and the regional offices.

Information material for all media can be obtained from WHO headquarters, Geneva, information units of the regional offices and United Nations information centres.

FOOD AND AGRICULTURE ORGANIZATION (FAO)

Freedom from want was proclaimed in the Atlantic Charter as one of the great peace aims; and even during the war no time was lost in preparing for international action in the post-war period. The objectives were to secure higher levels of nutrition and standards of living and more efficient production and distribution of agricultural products, as well as to improve the conditions of rural populations. The first of the war-time United Nations conferences called to make plans for international co-operation in specialized fields was that on Food and Agriculture, which met in May, 1943, at Hot Springs (United States).

ORGANIZATION

The conference set up an interim commission which drew up a constitution for the future United Nations Food and Agriculture Organization and submitted it to the governments. The first session of the FAO conference was convened at Quebec (Canada) where FAO came into being on 16 October 1945, when the constitution was signed by 42 governments.

On 7 November 1960, FAO had 81 members. Its conference—the policy-making body—meets bi-annually to plan the work of the organization and determine the level of the budget. Between sessions of the full conference, its affairs are reviewed by a council which is composed of representatives of 25 member governments. The Director-General, Mr. B. R. Sen, of India, is the chief administrator with authority over a secretariat of 1,300 international civil servants. The secretariat consists of a Technical Department, an Economics Department, and a Department of Public Relations and Legal Affairs, each under an Assistant Director-General, as well as a Programme and Budgetary Service and a Division of Administration and Finance. Within the Technical Department are divisions for land and water development, plant production and protection, animal production and health, rural institutions and services, fisheries, forestry and forest products, and nutrition. The Economics Department consists of divisions for commodities, statistics and economic analysis.

Regional and sub-regional offices are maintained in Accra (for Africa), Bangkok (for Asia and the Far East), Cairo (for the Near East), Mexico City (for Latin America, Northern Zone), Rio de Janeiro (for Latin America, Eastern Zone), Santiago (for Latin America), and Washington (for North America). About fifty national FAO committees serve as points of contact between the organization and governmental and non-governmental agencies.

FAO has its headquarters in Rome. Its bi-annual budget for 1960–61, as voted at the 1959 conference, amounts to nearly $19 million.

SHORTAGES AND SURPLUSES

Hunger, want, and the adequate supply of food are problems as old as the world. In modern times the two aspects of the problem—shortages and famine on the one hand, surpluses and lowered demand on the other, both causing economic difficulties, social crises and suffering— were joined together as a part of the over-all problem of economic development. By applying modern techniques to agriculture, the wealthier and more highly developed industrialized countries achieved spectacular increases in their output; not only are they able to provide their populations with sufficient quantities of varied food of high quality, but some of them also have large surpluses of staple foodstuff and agricultural raw material. On the other side, the poorer, under-nourished majority of mankind, retarded in its economic development, sees the gap widening: its numbers are increasing without a corresponding growth of food production, in either quantity or quality, and it has difficulty in marketing its export agricultural commodities at remunerative stabilized prices—indeed, there is often competition from the industrialized countries with a surplus of agricultural produce.

From the very beginning FAO has had to tackle the great problem of equitable distribution of foodstuff. After several proposals had failed to produce concrete action, the General Assembly of the United Nations in 1954 asked FAO to prepare a report on what had been done and what was being done to meet the objectives of raising the levels of production

147

and consumption, fighting chronic malnutrition, relieving famine, countering excessive price fluctuations, and promoting rational disposal of intermittent agricultural surpluses. A most interesting study, *Functions of a World Food Reserve*, was submitted to the United Nations and is under discussion by Ecosoc.[1]

In the meantime, studies were made and action was taken by FAO on the disposal and prevention of surpluses. A code of principles and guiding lines on surplus disposal has been worked out and adopted by many importing and exporting countries. The surpluses have been used to help population groups suffering from malnutrition, especially children and expectant mothers; to grant emergency relief in cases of crop failures and the resulting threat of famine; and to aid economic development. Pilot studies of practical measures for food surplus disposal have been made in several countries—e.g., distribution of skimmed milk in Egypt and Spain, utilization of surpluses for financing economic development in India.

In the field of commodities, FAO drafted the international olive oil agreement for a United Nations conference on the subject. Studies have been made on rice, cocoa, coconut, dairy products.

AGRICULTURE

The activities of FAO in particular fields—agriculture, forestry, fisheries, nutrition—are essentially of a technical nature, aimed at developing basic natural resources, at using improved methods of production and processing, at improving the agrarian structure, the training of technicians, and the establishment of essential government services.

In agriculture, one of the most important of FAO's jobs is to assist governments to appraise and improve soil and water resources within their countries. It conducts, in co-operation with the governments, soil surveys; and it promotes soil fertility improvement, the development of underground-water resources, the use of farm machinery, and improvement of farm implements. Emphasis is placed on an integrated approach to all these activities and on improving conditions of land tenure in order to provide incentives for the peasants and to strengthen the security of farm families on the land.

In other specialized fields, technical advice is given on plant production and protection, with particular attention to the breeding of national plants. International co-operation is promoted on a regional basis—in regard to rice in the Far East, maize in Europe, wheat and barley in the Near East. Seeds are distributed for experimental purposes, emphasis being laid on pastures and fodder production, as a basis for improved

---

1. See page 53.

animal husbandry and crop rotation. Regional campaigns have been organized to control major pests. FAO is playing a leading role in international action against locust invasions.

Control of animal diseases such as foot-and-mouth disease, rinderpest, etc., is becoming effective in many countries of Europe, Asia and elsewhere as government veterinary services are set up and a system established for rapid reporting of outbreaks, swiftly followed by vaccination and severe control measures. Regional co-operation between countries has been encouraged by FAO to make control measures more effective.

Animal production and health is one of FAO's major fields of operation. The constant effort is to promote better feeding and care and therefore better health and productivity of livestock and poultry.

Studies are made on agricultural credit facilities, farmers' co-operatives, handicraft and rural industries, measures to improve standards of rural welfare. Governments are advised concerning their agricultural education programmes. FAO has lately undertaken studies on the utilization of atomic energy in agriculture. Several papers on the use of radio-isotopes in plant growing, etc., were presented to the 1955 Atomic Conference and to more recent meetings, with the Atomic Energy Branch participating in seminars at Cambridge University in England and Cornell University in the United States during 1959.

FORESTRY AND FISHERIES

Sound exploitation of the world's timber resources and protection of forests is one of FAO's major concerns. It co-operates with the United Nations regional economic commissions in research and in studying the rational use of wood in industry and building, the marketing of timber, methods to increase the supply of pulp and paper and to find the raw material for their manufacture, the training of forest workers, and the spread of modern machinery.

FAO provides professional staff for the Timber Division of ECE and ECAFE.

The World's Forest Resources, published in 1955, the *Yearbooks of Forest Products Statistics*, and the series *World Forest Planting* are among the numerous publications on forestry and reforestation questions.

FAO's activities as regards fisheries—and fish is the main source of protein for tens of millions of people in Asia, Latin America and elsewhere—include advising and helping governments to set up fishery administrations and statistical and other government services to fisheries. Furthermore, FAO gives advice to governments on technical problems of fisheries development, including the introduction of mechanization and modern gear and equipment, improved methods of catching and processing fish, development of fish culture, and the improved handling, distribution and marketing of fish and fish products. Three regional fisheries councils—Mediterranean, Indo-Pacific, and Latin American—are especially concerned with problems of fisheries in their regions, one of the main ideas behind them being to promote international co-operation on a regional basis.

NUTRITION

Since FAO's basic aim is to increase food production and raise levels of nutrition throughout the world, a major responsibility of the Nutrition Division is to ensure that nutritional principles underlie the other activities of FAO, all of which have, or should have, one primary objective—namely, to ensure that people get enough of the right sort of food to eat. To attain this objective it is necessary to establish nutritional requirements, at least to the limited degree which current physiological knowledge makes possible, and to study and assess existing food consumption levels, this being the starting point for improvement.

In FAO's programme of work for 1958–59, the special 'functions' of the Nutrition Division were stated to be: '(a) the study and appraisal of food consumption on a world, regional and national basis, in order to assess the changes and developments in food production and supply needed for satisfactory nutrition; (b) the study of physiological requirements for calories and nutrients and the practical application of advancing knowledge of requirements; (c) the study and application of specific measures to ensure that effective use is made of available food supplies, with special reference to food technology, supplementary feeding and education in nutrition; (d) the improvement of family welfare, including family nutrition, through home economics education and extension programmes related to the real needs of populations; (e) direct assistance to governments in developing practical programmes in nutrition and home economics; (f) collaboration with other United Nations Agencies, in particular WHO and Unicef, which have special interest in certain aspects of nutrition.'

Among activities listed in this programme which may be specially mentioned are the attention given to education in nutrition and the assistance to governments in organizing proper feeding at school and in developing the production of protein-rich foods for mothers and children.

A joint FAO/WHO expert committee on nutrition meets periodically, as do regional committees for Asian and Latin American countries.

TECHNICAL ASSISTANCE

In all such activities the regular work of FAO is linked to its widespread activity in technical assistance. The FAO share in the funds of the Expanded Programme of Technical Assistance is larger than that of any other Specialized Agency—around 28.5 per cent. It has the largest number of experts in the field, actively collaborating in national programmes—more than 30 per cent of the total. In recent years (as in its early days), FAO has sent special missions to several countries, to meet requests for assistance in solving problems of developing or rehabilitating the local agriculture. Regular activities and those under technical assistance are now fully integrated, with an emphasis on regional projects. Desert locust control, grasslands and fodder improvement projects in the Near East, the Far East rice extension schemes, the Central American campaign to control foot-and-mouth disease, the development of the forest resources of the Amazon Basin—these are a few examples. Training centres for a variety of farm jobs, for dairy improvement, mechanization, irrigation, for improvement of rural social conditions, for co-operative land reform, for fisheries and forestry have been established in several regions and many countries. FAO participates in Unesco's centres for basic education and community development.[1]

On the national level emphasis is on training and schooling—the lack of trained staff in many underdeveloped countries is often the most serious obstacle to agricultural progress. Governments are also assisted in developing basic institutions: Ethiopia and Honduras were helped to establish agricultural administration, aid was given to Chile and Venezuela to develop sound forest legislation and create forestry schools and training centres on logging and timber grading. FAO efforts are centred on extending training facilities, organizing schooling groups, and awarding fellowships.

Typical of the larger national enterprises to develop resources are the paper and pulp project in Mexico, undertaken in co-operation with ECLA, and the exploitation of the water resources of Baluchistan as a basis of its agricultural development.

Special Fund.   As at the beginning of 1960, FAO had been assigned responsibility for 19 projects under the Special Fund, involving an amount of nearly $10 million with a further 13 projects likely to eventuate in the near future, involving another $6.5 million.

---

1. See page 117.

WORLD SEED CAMPAIGN

In 1957, FAO launched a world-wide campaign to promote the use of high quality seed of the best strains and varieties. By the beginning of 1960 the majority of member governments had decided to participate actively in this project, 74 of them (and their dependent territories) having taken positive action, either through newly-established National Seed Campaign Committees or through existing bodies.

According to the needs and facilities of their countries, National Seed Campaign Committees prepare national programmes which cover: introduction of improved crop and tree varieties; intensification of plant breeding and varietal research; multiplication of high quality stock seed; establishment of seed certification schemes; improvement of seed testing facilities; organization of seed distribution and trade and the adoption of seed acts, laws and regulations. Equal attention has been given to the means whereby the results of these activities can be brought to farmers, this being considered of special importance in countries where a gap exists between a very small nucleus of well-trained personnel, mostly educated abroad, and the comparative ignorance of the farmers themselves.

The World Seed Campaign is regarded as providing an excellent opportunity for mutual aid between member governments, and several have offered training facilities to other countries or regions which urgently need more qualified personnel for the development of their own seed campaigns. For example: Canada arranged a three-month course on seed improvement in 1959 for 11 trainees from eight Colombo Plan countries; and Sweden has arranged to organize during 1960 a seven-month International Training Centre on Genetics and Plant Breeding for 15 selected scholars to be recruited from Near and Middle East countries, and from India, Pakistan and Ceylon.

At the FAO conference in Rome in November 1959, it was decided to designate 1961 as 'World Seed Year'.

FREEDOM-FROM-HUNGER CAMPAIGN

In spite of 15 years of national and international effort, progress towards the goals set out in FAO's charter has been slow, and a world free from hunger is not yet in sight. Clearly, special efforts are called for. It was in this context that B. R. Sen, FAO's Director-General, saw the need for a world-wide campaign against hunger and want. Under the title 'Freedom-from-Hunger Campaign', the member nations of FAO adopted the project at their conference in November 1959. Broadly speaking, the activities of the campaign will be twofold: first, the promotion of a climate of opinion throughout the world in which the problems of hunger and want will be discussed, their causes analysed and remedies sought. This is an activity which will be most appropriately taken up by the more developed and prosperous countries. The second category of activity will include national and regional research and action projects designed to accelerate the tempo of development in underdeveloped countries and to secure increased production of food and better standards of nutrition.

The campaign will extend from 1960 through 1965, highlighted by a World Food Congress in 1963.

PUBLICATIONS AND PUBLIC INFORMATION

Publications of FAO now form an important library on agriculture and food problems. The basic works are the *world food surveys* of 1946 and 1952; since 1947 an annual report has been issued on the *State of Food and Agriculture*. More specialized are the *Yearbooks of Food and Agriculture Statistics*, and of *Forest Products Statistics*, and *Fishery Statistics*, supplemented by the monthly *Bulletin of Agricultural Economics and Statistics*, and a quarterly illustrated publication on forestry, *Unasylva*.

FAO's special studies, *The Efficient Use of Fertilizers*, and another, *Improving the World's Grasslands*, have become popular textbooks, reprinted commercially. Two substantial volumes which have been published commercially in London, with FAO providing all the text and illustrations, are *Fishing Boats of the World* and *Modern Fishing Gear of the World*. *World Food Problems* is the general title of a series of information pamphlets published on world food and agricultural problems and the attempts being made to solve them.

Much of FAO's information material serves a dual purpose: it informs the general public on the activities of the organization and—this applies particularly to audio-visual material, film and radio, filmstrips, exhibits —it is used as an auxiliary in its substantive work, in training centres, etc. It is available from the Public Information Service in Rome (now part of FAO's Department of Public Relations and Legal Affairs), from FAO's regional offices, and from United Nations information centres. In addition to regular press and radio releases about the organization's activities, the *FAO Bulletin* is published four times a year, and a *European Information Letter* also appears quarterly. Among other regular publications is the *World Seed Campaign News*.

The Work of FAO, the Director-General's report submitted to the conference, provides current information on the organization's work. In the present text several other basic publications, as well as some special studies, are mentioned: further information about these as well as about all other FAO publications—the range is a wide one—will be found in the catalogue which can be had from any sales agent (addresses are given on the back pages of publications), or direct from FAO, Rome.

The FAO Library is now a very extensive one, and is likely to prove of considerable interest not only to students of agriculture but also to journalists. FAO's Public Information Service now has 20,000 prints aavilable in its photograph library, and is willing to supply photographs as well as information and documentation to journalists who require them for the writing of articles, etc.

Course XIII

SPECIALIZED AGENCIES: TECHNICAL

INTERNATIONAL ATOMIC ENERGY AGENCY (IAEA)

The International Atomic Energy Agency (IAEA), a newcomer to the United Nations family, provides a striking example of progress in international co-operation and organization. IAEA was established to put atomic energy at the service of the progress and welfare of all the peoples of the world.

On 8 December 1953, President Eisenhower, addressing the United Nations General Assembly, urged the establishment of an international organization to 'serve the peaceful pursuits of mankind'.

In 1954 representatives of Australia, Belgium, Canada, France, Portugal, South Africa, the United Kingdom and the United States met in Washington to draft the Statute of such an organization. Representatives of Brazil, Czechoslovakia, India and the USSR joined this group in 1956.

A year after President Eisenhower's speech the United Nations General Assembly unanimously adopted a resolution calling for the establishment of the International Atomic Energy Agency which should 'seek to accelerate and enlarge the contribution of atomic energy to peace, health and prosperity troughout the world'.

Eightly-one nations participated in the Statute Conference held at United Nations Headquarters, New York, from 20 September to 26 October 1956. The Statute was unanimously approved and 70 States signed it on 26 October, the opening date for signature. Ten others signed within the next three months.

In July 1957, the Statute entered into force and the Agency came legally into being. The first General Conference (Vienna, 1 to 27 October 1957) approved a draft programme and budget for the Agency's first year (worked out by the 18 nations' preparatory commission established in 1956), elected 10 more States to the Board, in addition to the 13 members of the Board of Governors designated by the Preparatory Commission earlier.

Mr. P. Winkler (Czechoslovakia) was elected Chairman of the first Board. The conference also adopted a Relationship Agreement with the United Nations, approved the appointment of Mr. Sterling Cole (United States) as the Agency's first Director-General for a period of four years, and decided that the IAEA headquarters should be in Vienna (Austria).

ORGANIZATIONAL STRUCTURE

The International Atomic Energy Agency is an autonomous body forming part of the United Nations family of organizations and is accorded a 'leading position' in the international activities concerned with the peaceful use of the atom. It reports to the United Nations General Assembly and not to Ecosoc, as do the Specialized Agencies.

The three organs of the Agency are the General Conference, the Board of Governors and the secretariat headed by a Director-General. The governing bodies are the General Conference and the Board.

The General Conference consists of all members, at present numbering 73 (31 October 1960), each having one vote. It meets normally once a year and takes its decisions by majority vote, except on financial questions, amendments to the Statute and suspension from membership, requiring a two-thirds majority.

The General Conference elects 10 members of the Board (five members for a two-year term at each session), approves States for membership, considers the Board's annual report and approves reports for submission to the United Nations, and agreements with the United Nations and other organizations. It also approves the budget recommended by the Board and the appointment of the Director-General.

The Board of Governors consists of members designated or elected on a technological and regional basis. The Board carries out the functions of the Agency in accordance with the Statute and takes decisions by majority vote except on certain specific matters, such as the budget which requires a two-thirds majority. The Board meets approximately every third month, while its committees meet frequently.

The Director-General, as the chief administrative officer of the Agency, is responsible for the functioning, organization and appointment of the staff, under the authority of and subject to the control of the Board. There are five departments: Training and Technical Information; Technical Operations; Research and Isotopes; Safeguards and Inspection; Administration, Liaison and Secretariat.

The Agency has appointed seven eminent scientists to serve as a Scientific Advisory Committee, whose function is to advise on scientific and technical questions arising out of the Agency's programme.

FUNCTIONS AND ACTIVITIES

Assistance to Member States (missions, experts, equipment). IAEA assists its atomically less-developed members in drawing up or starting programmes for developing the peaceful uses of atomic energy.

In 1959 a preliminary assistance mission went to Burma, Indonesia, Thailand and Ceylon to study the requirements of these countries in respect of nuclear physics, raw materials, reactors, the agricultural and medical uses of isotopes and the training of nuclear personnel. Another such mission visited China (Taiwan), Japan, Korea, the Philippines and Viet-Nam and a third was sent to Argentina, Brazil and Venezuela. The fourth mission visited Afghanistan, Iran, Iraq, Turkey and Yugoslavia.

At the request of the governments concerned, fact-finding teams visited Pakistan, Thailand and the United Arab Republic in 1958. Similar teams visited Greece, Morocco and Tunisia in 1959.

Offers of consultants and experts have been made by technically advanced Member States. The Agency employs them both for fact-finding and preliminary assistance missions and for sending them on specific tasks to requesting countries.

Purchases and offers of nuclear equipment are also channelled through the Agency. In 1959, for instance, at the request of Brazil the Agency made equipment available for the national radiation measurement service.

Training of personnel. The training of nuclear scientists and technicians is another important task of IAEA, for little progress can be expected in the peaceful applications of atomic energy without an adequate number of technicians, scientists and teachers, particularly in the underdeveloped areas. In view of this the Agency from the very beginning started a programme under which nuclear science fellowships are awarded to persons from Member States for training at educational, scientific and research establishments in the atomically advanced countries. More than 300 fellowships are awarded annually.

International training courses on applications of radio-isotopes in medicine and agriculture are organized on a regional basis in close co-operation with some Specialized Agencies and the establishment of regional training centres is under study.

Mobile isotope laboratories are visiting Member States for training and demonstration purposes.

Exchange of specialists and visiting professors to give lectures on

157

nuclear science to students in Member States is being organized by IAEA.

SUPPLY OF FISSIONABLE AND SOURCE MATERIALS

One of the Agency's primary functions is to provide materials 'to meet the needs of research on, and development and practical application of, atomic energy for peaceful purposes, including the production of electric power, with due consideration for the needs of the underdeveloped areas of the world'.

To ensure the implementation of this function the Statute envisages that Member States which are in a position to do so make fissionable materials available to IAEA. At the Agency's first General Conference, offers of materials were made by the United Kingdom (20 kg. of uranium-235) and the United States (5,000 kg. of uranium-235). Source materials have been offered by Belgium (uranium), Canada (uranium), Ceylon (thorium ore), Czechoslovakia (uranium), India (thorium), Portugal (uranium concentrates), the Union of South Africa (uranium concentrates), and Spain (uranium concentrates).

Sources of supply are thus available to the Agency. The first request came from Japan for three tons of natural uranium for use in a research reactor. The uranium was given to the Agency by Canada free of charge and was then sold to Japan by the Agency for $35.50 per kg. Requests concerning the supply of enriched uranium to Austria and Finland are now under study. The paucity of requests must be seen against the slow development of power reactor programmes in most countries; it is confidently foreseen that the demands will increase sharply in the future.

PRODUCTION OF NUCLEAR POWER

The General Conference in 1958 recommended that the Agency 'initiate action for a survey of the needs of the less developed countries, with their consent, in the matter of nuclear generation plants suitable for their specific circumstances'.

The Agency is engaged on a programme in this field providing for studies of the technical suitability of available power reactors, studies of nuclear power costs, location of potentially promising situations and special action in training of power reactor specialists.

Data on the power situation in the interested countries are being classified and studied.

Full use is being made of the preliminary assistance missions mentioned above.

To help Member States in acquiring the most up-to-date view of the situation the Agency held a technical conference on the subject of small and medium power reactors in the late summer of 1960.

A detailed directory of power and research reactors has been published and will be folowed by directories on test and experimental reactors.

SCIENTIFIC AND TECHNICAL INFORMATION

By making its comprehensive scientific and technical library available to all Member States, IAEA contributes to making new material in the nuclear energy field more readily available to research workers, scientists and engineers throughout the world.

Scientific and technical conferences and symposia contribute very much to the exchange of information on the peaceful uses of nuclear energy among Member States and the Agency has initiated a series of such meetings.

The Agency's scientific publications also contribute to world-wide dissemination of nuclear energy information.

REGULATORY ACTIVITIES

The Agency attaches particular importance to the drafting of international rules and recommendations on health and safety standards and procedures.

A panel of experts, set up by the Agency, prepared a set of recommendations on the safe handling of radio-isotopes which was published in 1958 as a guide to isotope users.

Two panels are considering the establishment of satisfactory and uniform international standards for the safe transport of radio-active materials.

Studies are made on present methods for monitoring reactor accidents as well as on existing practices in the licensing of reactor operations.

The Agency also advises its members on various aspects of safety techniques and health protection.

Recommendations for adequate control of waste disposal in the sea are being studied by a panel of experts.

Under the Statute it is the Agency's task to 'establish and administer safeguards designed to ensure that special fissionable and other materials, services, equipment, facilities and information made available by the Agency or at its request or under its supervision or control are not used in such a way as to further any military purpose'.

The Board of Governors has already given its provisional approval to a set of general principles to be used in determining Agency safeguards to be applied to various types of assistance.

RESEARCH AND ISOTOPES

IAEA assists and advises its members on the application of radiation sources in agriculture, medicine and industry.

To encourage research IAEA awarded some fifty contracts to institutions in Member States. Several combined projects have also been prepared requiring close collaboration between institutes in more than one Member State, the work being co-ordinated by the Agency.

An *International Directory of Radio-isotopes* has been published.

A number of conferences and symposia dealing with research and isotopes have been organized and are planned for next year.

Research projects are undertaken by the Agency itself in relation to health and safety standards and safeguards. For this purpose a provisional laboratory has been equipped, consisting of a small chemical laboratory, a counting room for low activities, an electronics laboratory and a workshop. In 1959 the Agency started the construction of its functional laboratory which is expected to be in operation in early 1961. The Agency will then be in a position to carry out standardization of isotopes and preparation of radio-active standards; calibration and adaptation of measuring equipment; quality control of special materials for nuclear technology; measurements and analysis in connexion with the Agency's safeguards and health and safety programmes; and services to Member States.

It will be located near the laboratories and reactor of the Austrian Centre (Studiengesellschaft für Atomenergie) at Seibersdorf near Vienna and will be the first truly international laboratory in the world.

INTERNATIONAL CIVIL AVIATION ORGANIZATION (ICAO)

The war did not interrupt the development of air travel; on the contrary, with the tremendous expansion in the means of air transport brought about by military operations, it opened up great potentialities for civil aviation. Plans for organized international action in different fields of human activity which were drafted towards the end of the war included the establishment of an organization to guide and develop international civil aviation. At a conference of 52 nations, which met in Chicago in November 1944, the Convention on International Civil Aviation was adopted, providing for the creation of ICAO.

The organization began to function provisionally in August 1945, and came into being formally on 4 April 1947, the convention having been ratified by 26 States. The convention superseded two earlier agreements, the Paris Convention which established the International

Commission for Air Navigation, and the 1928 Havana Pan-American Convention on Commercial Aviation.

ORGANIZATION

The aim of ICAO is to encourage the development of airways, airports and air navigation facilities; to ensure safe, regular, efficient and economical air transport, eliminating discrimination between States and waste caused by unreasonable competitions; and to safeguard the rights and opportunities to operate international airlines.

The Assembly, the sovereign body of ICAO, elects a governing council of 21 members, which adopts international standards, recommends practices for air navigation and takes whatever steps are necessary to maintain the safety and regularity of operation of international air transport. Five field offices deal with regional questions: in Mexico City for North America and the Caribbean; in Lima for South America; in Paris for Europe and Africa; in Cairo for the Middle East; and in Bangkok for the Far East and the Pacific.

The net budget of ICAO for 1960 is $3,865,000 (Canadian). Eighty countries were members of ICAO on 30 November 1960. Its chief officers are: Walter Binaghi (Argentina), President of the Council, and Ronald M. Macdonnell (Canada), Secretary-General.

INTERNATIONAL STANDARDS

One of ICAO's principal functions is to secure uniformity, regularity and co-operation in the organization and maintenance of facilities and services necessary for international air transport. Fifteen sets of standards and recommended practices are in force, as annexes to the Convention on International Civil Aviation. These include: personnel licensing (licensing of operating and maintenance personnel); rules of the air (rules relating to visual and instrument flight); meteorology (codes, meteorological communications and meteorological services); aeronautical charts (standardization of charts for use in international aviation); dimensional units (to be used in air-ground communications; reduction in the variety of dimensional systems); operation of aircraft—international air transport (specifications which will ensure a level of safety above a prescribed minimum in similar operations throughout the world); aircraft nationality and registration marks (requirements for registration and identification of aircraft); airworthiness of aircraft (certification and inspection of aircraft according to uniform procedure); facilitation (reducing the red tape involved in border crossings); aeronautical telecommunications (standardization of communications systems and radio air navigation aids); air traffic services (establishment

161

and operation or air traffic control, flight information and alerting services); search and rescue (organization of facilities and services necessary for search and rescue); aircraft accident inquiry (uniformity in the notification, investigation of and reporting on aircraft accidents); aerodromes (characteristics and equipment for aerodromes used in international navigation); aeronautical information services (uniformity in methods of collection and dissemination of aeronautical information).

A State must notify ICAO of any differences between its own practices and those established by international standard.

CO-OPERATIVE MAINTENANCE OF FACILITIES

In areas of undetermined sovereignty or of sparse population where a single State cannot provide the necessary air navigation facilities, ICAO may make arrangements to provide financial or technical aid. One arrangement of this sort maintains nine floating ocean stations providing weather reports, communications, navigation and search and rescue facilities in the North Atlantic; 21 ships, owned or financed by 18 nations whose airlines fly across the ocean, service these nine stations. In addition, long-range radio navigation aid stations, air traffic control, telecommunications and meteorological services are 'jointly financed' in Iceland, Greenland and the Faroe Islands, and a transatlantic cable will be put into operation in 1962 between Canada and Scotland via Greenland and Iceland to help air traffic control.

International air law has been enriched by a Convention on the International Recognition of Rights in Aircraft, which is designed to secure recognition of property and other rights in aircraft even if they cross a frontier, and another on Damage caused by Foreign Aircraft to Third Parties on the Surface. The problem of nationality in an aircraft is under discussion; the nationality of a baby born in the air, the jurisdiction for a crime committed in an aeroplane, etc.

THE JET AGE

Ninety-six million people travelled by world airlines in 1959 and each was carried an average distance of 615 miles. In 1958, corresponding figures were 87 millions, each travelling an average of 606 miles.

ICAO's main preoccupation in the last few years has been the adaptation of international air navigation services to the requirements of the jet age, such as extending and reinforcing runways and improving upper-air weather information and navigation facilities. One method of providing the necessary facilities may be a large extension of joint financing activities.

TECHNICAL ASSISTANCE

ICAO participates in the United Nations Expanded Programme of Technical Assistance; the 1959 budget amounted to $1,450,000. Its services are much in demand in underdeveloped countries, which have jumped the era of railways and roads and are building up modern systems of air transport instead. Expert aid is given mostly to increase the safety and efficiency of air transport operations, in particular the development of ground services and the training of men in all the technical fields of aviation. ICAO is endeavouring to assist in overcoming three principal obstacles in the development of civil aviation; the lack of trained staff; inadequate administration due to lack of senior staff and insufficient means; and lack of equipment. The first two are, in the opinion of ICAO, the more important obstacles, and stress is being laid on training.

Missions of ICAO experts have been sent to 40 countries, and fellowships have been granted to nationals of 36 others.

REFERENCE

Memorandum on ICAO, a detailed description of the history, aims and activities of ICAO, can be had free of charge from the Public Information Office of ICAO, Montreal 3 (Canada).

INTERNATIONAL TELECOMMUNICATION UNION (ITU)

ORIGIN AND EVOLUTION

The International Telecommunication Union is the oldest of the intergovernmental organizations which have become specialized agencies in relation with the United Nations. It can thus claim to be the ancestor of the Specialized Agencies. It was born with the spread of the great invention of the nineteenth century, the telegraph, which rapidly crossed national frontiers to link major cities in Europe. International action was essential to establish an international telegraph network. It was necessary to reach agreement on the technical systems to be used, on uniform methods of handling messages, on the collection of charges. A procedure of international accounting had to be set up.

First came bilateral understanding between bordering countries, then international agreements between regional groups of countries, ending in an inter-European association. A truly international organization, open to all countries of the world, came into being in 1865 when the International Telegraph Union was created in Paris by the first International Telegraph Convention. This was the first important interna-

163

tional administrative organization, the members of which agreed to a set of basic telegraph service regulations. These were modified later as a result of practical operating experience. At Vienna, in 1868, a permanent international bureau was decided on and subsequently established in Berne.

The first regulations for the international telephone service were made in 1885. International services were progressively introduced between neighbouring countries, especially in Europe and North America. These services became world-wide in 1927 when radio provided a means of carrying the human voice across the ocean from continent to continent, but it was not until 1958 that agreement was reached on telephone regulations applicable to the entire world.

When, at the end of the nineteenth century, wireless (radiotelegraphy) became practicable, it was seen at once to be an invaluable complement to telegraphy by wire and cable, since radio alone could provide telecommunication between land and ships at sea. The first International Radio-telegraph Convention was signed in Berlin in 1906 by 27 maritime States. The International Radiotelegraph Conference in Washington in 1927 was a landmark in the development of radio, since it was at this conference that the Table of Frequency Allocations was first devised.

In 1932, two plenipotentiary conferences were held in Madrid: a Telegraph and Telephone Conference and a Radiotelegraph Conference. On that occasion the two existing conventions were amalgamated in a single International Telecommunication Convention and the countries which signed and acceded to it formed the International Telecommunication Union, replacing the International Telegraph Union. Four sets of regulations were annexed to the convention: telegraph, telephone, radio and the additional radio regulations.

A plenipotentiary conference which met in Atlantic City in 1947 to revise the Madrid convention introduced radical changes in the organization of the Union. New permanent organs of the Union were created for the Union, which became the Specialized Agency in relation to the United Nations in the sphere of telecommunication. Its headquarters were transferred from Berne to Geneva.

PURPOSES OF THE UNION

The purposes of the Union are to maintain and extend international co-operation for the improvement and rational use of telecommunication of all kinds; to promote the development of technical facilities and their most efficient operation with a view to improving the efficiency of telecommunication services, increasing their usefulness and making them, as far as possible, generally available to the public; and to harmonize the actions of nations in the attainment of those common ends.

STRUCTURE OF THE UNION

By the very nature of its work, the ITU has a very large membership—101 members and 5 associate members on 12 December 1960—including a number of territories which do not enjoy sovereign status.

The organization of the Union is as follows:

The Plenipotentiary Conference, which is the supreme organ of the Union;

Administrative conferences;

The Administrative Council;

The permanent organs of the Union, which are: the General Secretariat; the International Frequency Registration Board (IFRB); the International Radio Consultative Committee (CCIR); the International Telegraph and Telephone Consultative Committee (CCITT).

PLENIPOTENTIARY CONFERENCES

Meeting at intervals of normally not less than five years, the Plenipotentiary Conference determines the general policies for fulfilling the purposes of the Union. It reviews the work of the Union and revises the convention if it considers this necessary; in addition, it establishes the basis for the budget, determines a fiscal limit for the expenditure of the Union until the next conference, elects the members of the Union which are to serve on the Administrative Council, and elects the Secretary-General and the Deputy Secretary-General, etc. The last conference, which was held in Geneva in 1959, approved for the ordinary expenditure of the ITU during the years 1961 to 1965 an annual ceiling varying between 11 and 12.2 million Swiss francs.

ADMINISTRATIVE RADIO CONFERENCES

The basic task of the Administrative Radio Conferences is to revise the International Radio Regulations and to consider the incorporation therein of any agreements established since the previous conference. Among the actions taken by the Administrative Radio Conference, held in Geneva in 1959, the following are significant:

1. The radio frequency spectrum, in which various bands are allocated to the fixed, broadcasting, aeronautical mobile, land mobile, maritime mobile, radionavigation, radio-location, space, earth-space, radio astronomy, meteorological aids, amateur, standard frequency and time signal services, was re-apportioned up to 40,000 Mc/s according to the needs envisaged for the various services.

2. Allocations were made to new services which now require frequency allocations, in particular for space and earth-space research purposes

and for radio astronomy. As the future radio requirements for the use of outer space could not accurately be foreseen, the conference foresaw the convening of an Extraordinary Radio Conference to decide on the allocation of frequency bands for space radiocommunications purposes.

3. For certain bands of frequencies or services, in particular safety services, the plans adopted by previous conferences to assure the rational use of the frequency bands concerned were reviewed and amended pending the re-planning of the bands by future specialized conferences which were envisaged.

4. The duties of the International Frequency Registration Board were expanded.

5. In view of the difficulties experienced since 1947 in the preparation of long-term plans for the use of the high frequency broadcasting bands, a frequency management procedure was evolved for this service. In the future, administrations will notify to the IFRB projected seasonal schedules of their broadcasting services. The Board will integrate these schedules according to the principles of frequency management and publish them before the date upon which these schedules are to be put into operation.

6. Ways and means of relieving the pressure on the bands between 4 and 27.5 Mc/s—those mainly used for long distance or world-wide communications—are to be established. As a first step, the International Frequency Registration Board will study and analyse present usage with a view to determining those categories which might be satisfied by means other than the use of the high frequency bands, taking into account all pertinent facts, including those relating to the provision of economic assistance. Then a panel of experts will meet in 1961 and 1962 and will consider those uses which could be satisfied by other means, studying the implications involved. The panel will make a detailed report and recommend an agenda for a future conference to consider the policy decisions necessary to relieve pressure on the bands concerned.

The new radio regulations, signed by 83 members and 1 associate member, are to take effect on 1 May 1961.

ADMINISTRATIVE TELEGRAPH AND TELEPHONE CONFERENCE

The basic task of the Administrative Telegraph and Telephone Conference is to revise the International Telegraph Regulations and the International Telephone Regulations. Among the actions taken by the last Administrative Telegraph and Telephone Conference, which was held in Geneva in 1958, the following are significant:

1. The telephone regulations, as a whole, which were formerly appli-

cable solely to the European system, have been made of world-wide application.

2. The new telephone regulations contain basic provisions only, and make reference to CCITT recommendations for operational details. By adopting this new formula, the conference ensured that the telephone regulations will remain up to date for longer than would otherwise have been the case.

3. The telegraph regulations continue to include provisions concerning all aspects of the international telegraph service.

4. In accordance with a recommendation of the Plenipotentiary Conference held at Buenos Aires in 1952, the conference adopted an article stipulating a special tariff for prisoners of war and for civilians interned in war-time—Red Cross Telegram (RCT).

At the closing ceremony the revised telegraph regulations were signed by 64 countries and the telephone regulations by 61 countries. Both sets of revised regulations came into force on 1 January 1960.

ADMINISTRATIVE COUNCIL

The Administrative Council of the ITU is composed of 25 members of the Union elected by the Plenipotentiary Conference with due regard to the need for equitable representation of all parts of the world; it meets annually in Geneva and acts only in formal session. The Council is responsible for taking all steps to facilitate the implementation by the members and associate members of the Union of the provisions of the convention, of the regulations, of the decisions of the Plenipotentiary Conference and, where appropriate, of the decisions of other conferences and meetings of the Union.

GENERAL SECRETARIAT

The Secretary-General, G. C. Gross (United States), assisted by the Deputy Secretary-General, Dr. M. B. Sarwate (India), is responsible to the Administrative Council and to the Plenipotentiary Conference for all duties entrusted to the general secretariat and for all the administrative and financial services of the Union. The general secretariat provides the secretariats of conferences and undertakes secretarial work preparatory to, and following such conferences.

INTERNATIONAL FREQUENCY REGISTRATION BOARD (IFRB)

The essential duties of the IFRB are:

1. To effect an orderly recording of frequency assignments made by the different countries so as to establish, in accordance with the procedure

provided for in the radio regulations, and in accordance with any decisions which may be taken by competent conferences of the Union, the date, purpose and technical characteristics of each of these assignments, with a view to ensuring formal international recognition thereof.

2. To furnish advice to members and associate members with a view to the operation of the maximum practicable number of radio channels in those portions of the spectrum where harmful interference may occur.

3. To perform any additional duties, concerned with the assignment and utilization of frequencies, prescribed by a competent conference of the Union, or by the Administrative Council with the consent of the majority of the members of the Union in preparation for or in pursuance of the decisions of such a conference.

4. To maintain such essential records as may be related to the performance of its duties.

The Board consists of 11 independent members elected by the Administrative Radio Conference. It is assisted by a specialized secretariat.

At the Administrative Radio Conference, held in Geneva in 1959, the duties of the Board were expanded considerably in respect of the examination, recording and co-ordination of the frequency assignments of the radio stations of the world, of affording more effective assistance to new and developing countries in the establishment of their radio services, and of securing in the future the more effective use of the radio frequency spectrum. The Board was also entrusted with the technical planning for future radio conferences, particularly the panel of experts (see under 'Administrative Radio Conference').

INTERNATIONAL CONSULTATIVE COMMITTEES

The duties of the International Radio Consultative Committee (CCIR) are to study technical and operating questions relating to radiocommunication and to issue recommendations on them.

The duties of the International Telegraph and Telephone Consultative Committee (CCITT) are to study technical, operating and tariff questions relating to telegraphy and telephony and to issue recommendations on them.

In performing its duties, each consultative committee pays due attention to studying questions and formulating recommendations directly connected with the establishment, development and improvement of telecommunication in new or developing countries in both the regional and international fields. At the request of the countries concerned, each consultative committee may also study and offer advice concerning their national telecommunication problems.

The administrations of all members and associate members of the Union are, of right, members of the consultative committees. Any recognized private operating agency may also be a member with the approval of the member or associate member of the Union which has recognized it. Each consultative committee works through the medium of the Plenary Assembly, which meets normally every three years; study groups set up by the Plenary Assembly to deal with questions to be examined; a director elected by the Plenary Assembly; a specialized secretariat, which assists the director; and laboratories or technical installations set up by the Union.

The director of the CCIR is Mr. E. R. Metzler (Switzerland) and the director of the CCITT is J. Rouvière (France).

TECHNICAL ASSISTANCE

The work of the consultative committees and of the International Frequency Registration Board is a form of technical assistance to members of the ITU. The Union also participates in the Expanded Programme of Technical Assistance, working out programmes in the field of telecommunications, supervising the activities of experts, organizing fellowship groups.

Economic development creates the need for communications, for telegraph and telephone services not only for domestic use, but also to improve connexions with the outer world. The ITU is asked to help in the planning of trunk lines connecting isolated areas; in improving existing services and developing new services; in maintaining and modernizing equipment. Lack of skilled labour and operating specialists is one of the principal handicaps to developing telecommunication services, and the ITU concentrates on training in its technical assistance work.

REFERENCE AND DOCUMENTATION

CODDING, L. A., Jr. *The Telecommunication Union.* Leiden, 1952. A detailed study of the organization and activities of the ITU.

UNIVERSAL POSTAL UNION (UPU)

The Universal Postal Union (like ITU, 10 years its senior) was born of the urgent need—arising from the growing flow of international mail—to base exchange of mails on sound agreements respected by all countries. The Union was formally established in July 1875, with the coming

169

into force of the Universal Postal Convention, adopted at a Postal Congress in Berne.

ORGANIZATION

UPU unites all its members in a single postal territory for the reciprocal exchange of mails. The first postal convention already guaranteed freedom of transit throughout the whole territory of the Union; it introduced arbitration to settle differences; it established a set of rules for rates, charges, collection of dues and payments.

The original convention was subsequently extended and improved, and, until July 1948, any country could join it by a simple unilateral declaration of accession. Except for a few isolated areas, the entire world is included in UPU postal territory; its membership was 100 on 11 December 1960. Its seat is in Berne (Switzerland), and the budget of UPU amounts to 2.5 million Swiss francs annually.

The objectives of UPU as defined in the Berne Convention are essentially the same as nearly a century ago, when the treaty was concluded: the organization and improvement of the various postal services and promotion of international collaboration in this domain. Every five years international postal congresses meet to review and to perfect the Union's system. Special technical questions are dealt with by committees of delegates of postal administrations.

The Congress of UPU which was held at Ottawa in 1957 set up a permanent commission, called the Consultative Commission for Postal Studies (CCEP), open to all Member States of the Union and charged with carrying out studies and issuing opinions on matters affecting the postal service. To direct and co-ordinate its activities, the commission elects among its own members an administrative council of 20 members, chosen on the basis of equitable geographical distribution, and divided into three sections dealing with questions of technique, development and economics.

By now the various instruments worked out and adopted by postal congresses, in addition to the Universal Postal Convention and provisions concerning letter post, consist of eight supplementary agreements: on insured letters and boxes, parcels, money orders and postal travellers' cheques, postal transfers, each on delivery, postal debt collection, international post office savings banks, subscriptions for newspapers and periodicals.

In 1947 a new organ of UPU was created, the Executive and Liaison Committee of 20 members elected by the Congress, which meets once a year at the headquarters of the Union, between the congresses.

THE INTERNATIONAL BUREAU

Functions of the secretariat of UPU are performed by the International Bureau, which is the permanent, central organ of the Union, the centre of consultations and information for member countries.

The principal task of the Bureau is to collect and publish information which postal administrations have to communicate to each other, and to carry out investigations, consultations, and documentary work which members ask it to undertake. It acts also as a clearing house in settling accounts connected with international postal services.

The Bureau publishes a monthly bulletin in seven languages, *Union Postale* containing relevant information for national administrations. The Bureau is headed by its director, Dr. Fritz Hess, of Switzerland.

WORLD METEOROLOGICAL ORGANIZATION (WMO)

Weather does not respect national frontiers and WMO, established 'with a view to co-ordinating, standardizing and improving the exchange of meteorological information on a world-wide scale in the aid of human activities' has the largest membership of all the Specialized Agencies— 108 members on 11 December 1960.

ORGANIZATION

WMO grew out of the International Meteorological Organization, an organization of national weather services created more than eighty years ago. The convention of WMO provided that members of the organization would be States and territories maintaining their own weather services. A World Meteorological Congress, the policy-making body of WMO, meets every four years. The director of the weather services of each member is normally the principal delegate of each delegation. An executive committee meeting once a year directs the work of WMO. WMO's secretariat is headed by D. A. Davies (United Kingdom) and co-ordinates both the technical and administrative activities of the organization. Its seat is at Geneva. WMO's current budget is $2,694,000 for four years, 1960–63, to meet ordinary expenses.

Six regional meteorological associations—for Africa, Asia, South America, North and Central America, South West Pacific, and Europe— are responsible for solving regional problems and making practical regional arrangements.

Eight technical commissions study the basic problems of world-wide co-operation in meteorology and the various applications of meteorology to human activities and make recommendations in their respective fields:

commissions for agricultural meteorology, maritime meteorology, aeronautical meteorology, hydrological meteorology, synoptic meteorology, aerology, climatology, instruments and methods of observation.

WEATHER REPORTS

The international exchange of weather reports is one of the essential tasks of WMO. Following internationally agreed methods and practices, which are practically uniform everywhere, observers at weather stations throughout the world make meteorological observations at exactly the same time, at regular intervals. Every day about 8,000 land stations and 3,000 ships transmit 100,000 weather observations for the surface of the earth and a large number of special stations, transport and reconnaissance aircraft provide information relating to the upper air. This work is governed by *Technical Regulations*, a series of handbooks and schedules, which contain international rules concerning observing stations, forecasting practices, services for shipping and agriculture, telecommunications and air traffic and lists of weather stations of the world.

Assistance to less developed areas of the world is rendered in the framework of the United Nations Technical Assistance Programme. Thirty-four countries secured assistance in 1959 in establishing or developing their national meteorological services and in making use of the knowledge of weather in their economic life.

WMO collaborates with the United Nations in the water resources development programme. Training seminars on flood forecasting and other hydrological problems were held by WMO in 1957 and 1959. With Unesco, WMO co-operates in the arid lands and humid tropics research projects. It has contributed to the studies made on the use of natural energy resources—wind and solar energy.

WMO collaborates with FAO in the field of meteorological service for agriculture, forestry and fisheries, and with ICAO in the field of aeronautical meteorology.

INTERNATIONAL GEOPHYSICAL YEAR

The meteorological observations taken during the International Geophysical Year 1957–58 constitute a large part of the whole amount of data collected during this unprecedented scientific programme.

A special meteorological data centre was set up by WMO to collect the weather observations made during the International Geophysical Year. Approximately 13 million observations have been collected and are being published in the form of microcards. The total collection is expected to contain about 16,000 cards, containing data of great importance for the study of the motion of the atmosphere over the whole earth.

METEOROLOGY IN THE FIGHT AGAINST THE DESERT LOCUST

The use of weather information and climatological data in the fight against invasions of desert locust swarms was furhter explored by a technical assistance mission of WMO in British East Africa. Meteorological elements play an important role in relation to the breeding and movements of locust swarms. Meteorological maps were prepared for a chosen period of one year and the mission started in 1959 to establish the correlation of these weather charts with charts of locust movements. Since this is the first time that complete meteorological maps have been plotted for a considerable area extending both north and south of the Equator, it is expected that valuable results will also be obtained from this work which will improve weather forecasting in the tropics.

ATOMIC ENERGY AND METEOROLOGY

WMO has established a panel of experts to give advice on meteorological aspects of the application of radio-active isotopes and of the peaceful uses of atomic energy.

Air pollution which may be caused by gaseous radio-active wastes constitutes a potential danger to health and safety, in particular in connexion with reactor accidents, and in this respect meteorological techniques for the evaluation and prediction of atmospheric diffusion are of great importance. In co-operation with the United Nations, WMO has also dealt with the transport and removal by the atmosphere of radio-active debris from nuclear tests.

The third World Meteorological Congress in April 1959 reviewed the meteorological aspects of atomic energy and decided that the organization can play a useful role in the use of radio-isotopes for meteorological measurements; the safety of atomic plants; and the measurement of air and water radio-activity.

ARTIFICIAL SATELLITES AND METEOROLOGY

A panel of experts has been established by WMO to examine this subject. It has recommended that WMO should encourage the international exchange of meteorological information obtained from satellites, and in particular give urgent consideration to the most effective way of disseminating storm warnings based on this information.

The first results of observations from satellites will be mainly of use for research purposes, but operational applications may not be far behind. In particular, it may be possible to detect the development of severe storms at an early stage in areas where this is at present difficult owing to the sparsity of regular weather reporting stations over the oceans and in areas where there are few inhabitants. Such information could be of great value to weather forecasters.

PUBLICATIONS

Publications of WMO include technical notes, nomenclatures and guides, and the quarterly *Bulletin of WMO*. The organization has also published an *International Cloud Atlas* in several volumes, one of which contains 121 black and white and 103 coloured photographs of all types of clouds.

REFERENCE AND DOCUMENTATION

WMO Bulletin. Geneva. A quarterly publication. In addition to data of interest to professional meteorologists, it contains articles of general interest to the public.
WMO Annual Report to members of the organization and to the United Nations.

INTERGOVERNMENTAL MARITIME CONSULTATIVE ORGANIZATION (IMCO)

The twelfth, and the youngest, Specialized Agency of the United Nations came into being on 17 March 1958, when 21 States, seven of them having a total of at least 1 million tons of commercial shipping each, became parties to a convention adopted at a conference in Geneva in February-March 1948.

The aims of this Agency, IMCO, are to provide machinery for co-operation among governments in the field of governmental regulations and practices concerning technical matters of shipping engaged in international trade, and to encourage the general adoption of the highest standards for maritime safety and efficiency in navigation.

Te convention specified further that it shall discourage discriminatory action and restrictions by governments affecting international shipping; that it shall provide for exchange of information, and generally take up any shipping matters referred to it by any organ of the United Nations.

ORGANIZATION

The Assembly of IMCO, the policy-making body, meets every two years. The executive body, the Council, consists of 16 members, of whom eight represent countries furnishing international shipping services, and eight represent those having a significant interest in international seaborne trade. A Maritime Safety Committee of 14 members is elected by the Assembly from among nations having an important interest in maritime safety, of which at least eight are the largest ship-owning nations. The first Assembly of IMCO was held in London in January 1959, and was attended by representatives of 31 nations. It elected its Council members for 1959–61, consisting of Argentina, Australia, Belgium, Canada, France, the Federal Republic of Germany, Greece, India, Italy, Japan, the Netherlands, Norway, Sweden, the USSR, the United Kingdom and the United States.

Ove Nielsen, Denmark, was elected Secretary-General of the organization. Its headquarters were established in London. On 17 November 1960, there were 43 members of IMCO.

A difference of opinion arose over the election of members of the Maritime Safety Committee. The Assembly failed to agree on the interpretation of the convention stating that 'this committee shall consist of 14 members having an important interest in maritime safety, of which not less than eight shall be the largest ship-owning nations . . .'. Panama and Liberia contended that they were entitled to election under this category, but their view was not accepted by the Assembly.

The Assembly elected as the 'largest ship-owning nations' the United States, the United Kingdom, Norway, Japan, Italy, the Netherlands, France and the Federal Republic of Germany. Six additional nations were nominated: Argentine, Canada, Greece, Pakistan, the United Arab Republic and the USSR. Several countries, including the United States, contested the validity of the election, and the Assembly, in view of the disagreement over the interpretation of the clause, decided to refer the matter to the International Court of Justice for an advisory opinion.

The Assembly approved the agreement concerning the relationship of the Agency with the United Nations and ILO and agreed to accept duties in connexion with the International Convention for the Safety of Life at Sea, for the prevention of pollution of the sea by oil, and the International Code of Signals, and the unification of tonnage measurement of ships.

The budget of IMCO for 1959–61 was fixed at $726,000.

The second Assembly of IMCO will be held in the spring of 1961 in London.

Course XIV

SPECIALIZED AGENCIES: FINANCIAL AND ECONOMIC

In the field of international financing three Specialized Agencies are now active: the International Bank for Reconstruction and Development, the International Monetary Fund, and the International Finance Corporation.

A United Nations Monetary and Financial Conference of 44 countries met at Bretton Woods (USA) during the war, in July 1944, to lay plans for international economic and financial co-operation in post-war years. Two international institutions were created, the International Bank for Reconstruction and Development and the International Monetary Fund. The International Finance Corporation was formed in 1956 to complement the activities of the International Bank for Reconstruction and Development.

INTERNATIONAL BANK FOR RECONSTRUCTION AND DEVELOPMENT (BANK)

The World Bank was established with the purpose of providing and facilitating international investment for increasing production, for promoting international trade, and for raising living standards. Its function is to assist the international flow of capital for productive projects, and to aid its member nations in the development of their industry, agriculture, and public services. Lending money for these purposes is the Bank's chief activity.

The Bank started operations in June 1946. The 66 member countries of the Bank are its stockholders, each having subscribed a part of the total capital. The highest authority of the Bank is the Board of Governors, one governor for each Member State. Each State has 250 votes, plus one vote for each share of capital stock held.

The Board of Governors, which meets annually, has delegated most of its powers to the Board of Executive Directors, five of whom are appointed by the five members with the largest number of shares, and 13 elected by governors who represent the remaining members. Each director casts the number of votes of the member, or group of members, by whom he was elected or appointed. The Executive Directors select the President of the Bank, who is the Chief Executive Officer of the Bank. This is currently Eugene R. Black, of the United States. He heads an international staff of about 650.

CAPITAL STRUCTURE

When the Bank was established, its authorized capital was $10 billion. Of this, only 20 per cent was paid in by member countries, partly in gold and partly in their national currencies; 80 per cent remained on call and served to support the Bank in its borrowing operations. In September 1959, the authorized capital was increased to $21 billion and each member was asked to double its subscription, the additional capital to remain on call. The effect was to provide massive additional guarantee resources to serve as backing for the Bank's sales of bonds and notes to investors. As a result of this and other special increases in subscription made by some members, the Bank's subscribed capital rose to approximately $18.8 billion by 31 March 1959.

LENDING OPERATIONS

Bank loans can be granted to Member States directly, or to public or private enterprises in the territories of Member States, in which case the loans must be guaranteed by the respective governments. The Bank carefully studies the economic and financial position of the borrowing country before granting a loan. It examines on the spot the economic and technical soundness of the projects, which have to meet an important economic need. The loans normally provide the foreign exchange needed to import equipment, material, and services for the projects financed by the Bank. Other costs must be met locally.

The first loans were made to several war-damaged European countries —reconstruction credits for purchase of equipment and supplies. Later, emphasis shifted to loans financing projects for developing industry, agriculture, transport, and natural resources of less developed member countries.

As of 30 June 1959, the gross total of loans granted amounted to $4,426 million, meeting basic needs of more than fifty countries in all the continents ($589 million for Africa, $1,297 million for Asia, $318 million for Australia, $1,288 million for Europe, $934 million for Latin America). A total of $3,377 million was actually disbursed. All the loans, except for $500 million in 1947 for reconstruction, are for development purposes. More than half the money lent was for transportation facilities and electric power generation and distribution. Transport loans financed some fifty road, port, railway and other transport prospects and the expansion of three international airlines. More than $300 million was lent for agricultural projects such as irrigation and flood control, land improvement, farm mechanization and crop processing and storage.

The rate of interest, including a 1 per cent commission allocated to a special reserve is now 6 per cent. Borrowers have met all payments of principal and interest due.

Funds for lending. The main sources of financing the Bank's lending operations are the paid-in capital and the funds derived from the sales of the Bank's bonds and other borrowings in the world's investment markets. On 30 June 1959, the Bank had available the equivalent of about $1.5 billion from its capital and about $1.9 billion from borrowings in various currencies. The holders of the Bank's bonds are pension and trust funds, insurance companies and savings banks, commercial banks and private investors all over the world.

The Bank also increases its fund for lending purposes by selling parts of its loans to investors. Loans are also made in participation with private investors.

The gross total of funds lent or available for lending as of 30 June 1959, from capital, bonds, loans sold, repayments of loans and other operations, amounted to some $4.5 billion.

Income and expenditure. The Bank derives its income from interest on loans, commissions, and investments. The income from commissions is appropriated to a Special Reserve to meet the Bank's liabilities on its borowings and guarantees. It amounted to $138 million on 30 June 1959. The gross income for 1958–59, exclusive of commissions, was $122 million, from which administrative expenses, interest on borrowings and other financial expenses were met, leaving a net earning of $46.5 million, which was added to the Supplemental Reserve against losses on loans. This reserve totals $282 million. Administrative expenses were $9,750,000 in 1958–59.

ADVISORY AND TECHNICAL ASSISTANCE

In addition to banking operations the Bank provides various forms of advisory services to its members. Several States have asked for missions to survey their economics and to help to formulate programmes of investments and priorities, to recommend improvements in the governments' financial and economic policies, etc.

The Economic Development Institute, a staff college organized by the Bank in 1955, runs courses for senior officials with a view to helping to raise the standards of economic management, to publish studies on development problems, etc.

The Bank is not a direct participant in the Expanded Programme of Technical Assistance, but it is represented on the Technical Assistance Board and co-operates with other Specialized Agencies in their technical assistance activities.

The Bank acted as fiscal agent of the United Nations for the funds contributed by various governments towards the cost of the clearance of the Suez Canal in 1957. It also greatly contributed, as mediator, to the settlement of the terms of compensation to be paid by the United Arab Republic as a consequence of the nationalization of the Suez Canal, and of the financial claims of the United Kingdom and the United Arab Republic which arose out of the Suez incident. The Bank is also engaged in helping to settle the dispute between India and Pakistan over sharing the waters of the Indus Basin.

INTERNATIONAL MONETARY FUND (FUND)

The Fund, as already mentioned, was established at Bretton Woods together with the World Bank. Its aims, as stated in its Articles of Agreement, are to promote international monotary co-operation, to facilitate the expansion and balanced growth of international trade, to promote exchange stability, and to assist in the establishment of a multilateral system of payments free of exchange restrictions. The Fund has now 66 members who—with the exception of Cuba and the Dominican Republic—are also members of the Bank. Each member is assigned a quota expressed in United States dollars, which determines the voting strength and the subscription of the members, as well as the amount of foreign exchange which they may purchase from the Fund.

The authorities of the Fund are organized on the same pattern as those of the Bank. The Managing Director is Per Jacobsson, of Sweden, heading an international staff of 400. The administrative expenses are covered by income from operational charges and from investments.

HOLDINGS OF THE FUND

Assets of the Fund consist of subscriptions by its members. Subscriptions —equal to the quotas—are payable partly in gold, up to 25 per cent, and partly in member's currency. In 1959 the capital of the Fund was increased from the original $9,211 million to $14,325 million, in the expectation of its being able to play a bigger part in reinforcing its members' reserves and in the move towards convertibility of national currencies. Quotas ranged, before the increase of capital, from as low as $500,000 for Panama to $1,300 million for the United Kingdom (now $1,950 million) and $2,750 million for the United States (now $4,125 million). Gold holdings of the Fund are stored in a number of central banks. The part of subscription in member currencies is deposited in the central bank in each member country.

EXCHANGE TRANSACTIONS

Financial assistance to its members is a vital part of the Fund's functions. It is intended to help members to face balance of payments problems of a temporary nature by reinforcing their monetary reserves while they take the necessary corrective measures.

These exchange transactions take the form of a member's purchase from the Fund of needed foreign currency for an equivalent amount of the member's own currency. Members may also obtain stand-by arrangements, which assure drawings upon the resources of the Fund up to specific limits and over a period not exceeding one year.

This 'purchased' currency is expected to be repaid ('repurchased') within a period not exceeding three to five years, or reduced by the purchase of the member's currency by another member. A member is obliged to repurchase his currency when his monetary reserves improve. A service charge of one half per cent is made for the sale of currency and for the stand-by arrangements.

Purchases and stand-by arrangements were particularly heavy in 1956 and 1957, when, for a 12-month period, drawings amounted to $1 billion. The total now exceeds $3.4 billion. The Fund's assistance is asked not only to meet foreign exchange deficits, but also to form a reserve against speculation and emergency, to build a defence of a country's currency, and to help its stabilization.

Free convertibility of the currencies of all the members of the Fund being one of the major objectives of its activities, the Fund's transactions are also meant to assist in the establishment and maintenance of convertibility. The Fund publishes regularly a list of official par values of the currencies of its members, expressed in gold and United States dollars. Establishment of these values, revisions, and changes are made in consultation with the Fund. Members of the Fund have agreed not to change the value of their currencies more than 10 per cent without consulting the Fund.

The Fund keeps under review the financial and monetary conditions of member countries, who supply it with relevant information. *Inter-*

national Financial Statistics, a monthly publication of the Fund, is a most informative magazine on the world's economic and financial situation.

INTERNATIONAL FINANCE CORPORATION (IFC)

The need to create other means for financing the economic development of underdeveloped countries, in order to supplement the activities of the Bank, has been repeatedly stressed in the Economic and Social Council in the course of its debates. To meet the need of capital for productive private ventures, the idea was launched of establishing an international corporation to deal directly with private businessmen and investors and help facilitate the financing of private enterprises.

The Corporation was formed on 24 July 1956, when 31 countries, with a capital subscription totalling $78 million, completed legislative action authorizing them to become members of the Corporation. The Corporation had 58 members on 3 December 1960. Their subscription is $95 million, authorized by the Articles of Agreement, which are the constitutional basis of the Corporation. Membership of the IFC is open only to members of the Bank and the Fund. It has its headquarters in Washington, in the building of the Bank, and is served by an international staff of 65. R. L. Garner, of the United States, the president of the Executive Board of the IFC is also its chief executive officer. Administrative expenses are covered by income from subscribed capital and from investments; gross earnings for 1958–59 amounted to $3,500,000, net income was $1,740,000.

HOW IT OPERATES

The purpose of the IFC being to further economic development by investing, without government guarantee, in productive private enterprises, the Corporation deals directly with private business and finances private enterprises only. It does not seek and does not accept any government guarantee. It judges projects on their merits as investment for private capital and concentrates on projects in less developed countries. IFC is essentially an investing, rather than a lending institution. Its investments are not conventional, fixed interest loans. They are intermediate between debt and equity, that is loans carrying interest, plus options on share capital, rights to participate in the growth of the business, or a combination of both. The Corporation intends to revolve its funds by selling the investments, as soon as they prove sufficiently successful to attract private investors.

In the first three years of existence the IFC financed 28 projects in 13 countries totalling $24 million, among others an electric equipment

181

plant in Brazil, a machine tool factory in Mexico, a copper and smelting enterprise in Chile, an Australian timber-processing plant, and a cotton textile factory in Pakistan. It is not intended to exceed $2 million of investment in any single project. In most cases it is not practical for IFC to make an investment in enterprises which will have total assets of less than about $500,000 or the equivalent. Generally, an IFC investment does not exceed $2 million to $3 million. Larger investments are considered in special cases, particularly where IFC's participation will serve to attract private capital. Investments of less than about $100,000 are not ordinarily considered.

All of IFC's capital is in United States dollars, but the Corporation is prepared to denominate its investments, at least in part, in other currencies if justified by their stability and by the other terms of the investment. It is estimated that every dollar invested by the IFC has been accompanied by 3.5 dollars of industrial and private capital.

GENERAL AGREEMENT ON TARIFFS AND TRADE (GATT)

GATT is not a Specialized Agency of the United Nations; it is a close relation of the United Nations family, due to the fact that it was established pending the formation of an International Trade Organization. Today GATT has close working relations with the United Nations Secretariat and with the secretariats of certain Specialized Agencies; GATT has statutory relations with the International Monetary Fund.

In 1946, Ecosoc decided to call an International Conference on Trade and Employment with a view to creating an international trade organization. When they met in Geneva in 1947, members of the preparatory committee, which was set up to draft the convention of the organization, decided to negotiate between themselves to obtain tariff reductions and to agree on a set of trade rules which would guarantee that these reductions would not be frustrated by the creation of other artificial barriers. The results of these negotiations were embodied in an understanding called the General Agreement on Tariffs and Trade, with 23 original signatories. GATT entered into force on 1 January 1948.

The United-Nations-sponsored conference on international trade met in Havana in 1947–48 and adopted the Charter of the International Trade Organization (ITO)—an ambitious and far-reaching instrument—to promote and regulate the world-wide exchange of goods, and multilateral trading between nations. The Havana Charter was still-born. By the end of 1950 it became evident that the main trading nations—and the United States in particular—would not accede to ITO. Thus GATT remained the only world-wide agreement dealing with questions of international trade.

GATT is not an organization; it has no charter or statutes, but the Agreement specifies that the parties to it shall meet from time to time for consultations. These meetings of the member governments have taken place regularly since 1949, and GATT has been gradually built into an international institution.

Thirty-seven countries are now parties to the Agreement, and five more are closely associated. At each session of the contracting parties a number of countries attend as observers. Eighty-five per cent of world trade is represented by the parties to GATT.

To assist and facilitate negotiations, to service meetings of the contracting parties, a secretariat of 60 has been formed, with Eric Wyndham White as Executive Secretary, located in Geneva.

A CODE OF INTERNATIONAL COMMERCIAL RULES

GATT is a contractual agreement and its rules are contractual obligations of the signatory parties. The tariff concessions agreed upon in the course of the 1947 Geneva negotiations were incorporated in the Agreement in its essential Article II, next to the first article on the application of the most-favoured nation clause. Most of the other provisions of the Agreement are linked to the tariff concessions, and contain a number of obligations to prevent trade measures which would affect the benefits derived from concessions made in tariff rates. A code of rules of commercial policy has thus been created, and the sessions of GATT have become a place for discussion on international trade policies.

Three main tariff negotiations followed those of Geneva in 1947. The results of these negotiations were embodied in the Agreement. Tariff rates for tens of thousands of items entering into the world's commerce have been reduced or stabilized.

The sessions are now held twice a year, usually in Geneva, and are concerned with questions arising out of the operation of GATT, or which are brought up as complaints of violation of the Agreement's rules of fair trading. Complaints made under the Agreement may never reach the stage of discussion, because they may be settled through direct consultations between governments. The review of complaints in the meetings has often led to direct agreement, or to the opening of consultations. Where a settlement cannot be reached rapidly, the complaint is held under review for several sessions.

REVIEW OF INTERNATIONAL TRADE ARRANGEMENTS

GATT sessions also serve for a review of trends and developments in international commercial policies, as happened in 1957 when, in accordance with the terms of the Agreement, the Rome Treaty establishing the European Economic Community—popularly known as the European Common Market—was submitted to the contracting parties for consideration. In 1960 they will consider—in relation to GATT obligations—the convention establishing the European Free Trade Association (the 'Outer Seven') and probably, the newly-formed free trade area in Latin America.

During a general review of international trade which took place in 1957, attention was drawn in particular to the growing share in exports of the industrialized countries and the failure of the underdeveloped areas to maintain their relative position. The decline in the prices of primary products, and growing agricultural protection were also stressed. It was decided to appoint a panel of experts to examine current trends and to assess prospects of international trade. On the basis of their report a programme for trade expansion was launched. As part of this drive there will be a further general round of negotiations for the reduction of tariff levels, opening at Geneva in September 1960. An examination of agricultural policies is being made with the aim of lessening the harmful effects of agricultural protectionism in international trade, and a special inquiry is being undertaken into the difficulties which face the expansion of trade of the less developed countries, with a view to increasing the export earnings of these countries.

ORGANIZATION FOR TRADE CO-OPERATION

In 1954, during a review of GATT in the light of seven years' experience, the contracting parties drew up an agreement which would establish a permanent organization to be called the Organization for Trade Co-operation, to administer GATT on a permanent basis, sponsor international trade negotiations, and serve as a forum for discussion of problems of international commerce. The organization will be formed when accepted by governments whose foreign trade accounts for 85 per cent of the total external trade of the contracting parties. So far the United States has not agreed to join the proposed organization and therefore it has not been brought into being.

REFERENCE AND DOCUMENTATION

GATT publications include an annual report, *International Trade,* since 1952: this reviews world trade developments, and describes the work of GATT. Publications of general interest include a series of addresses by the Executive Secretary: *The Achievements of GATT, The First Ten Years of GATT,* and *International Trade; Challenge and Response*—all available free from the secretariat. A year by year account of GATT's work will be found in the United Nations *Yearbook.*

Course XV

REPORTING AND DISSEMINATING INFORMATION ON THE UNITED NATIONS

The Office of Public Information of the United Nations and the information services of the Specialized Agencies were created to meet the demand for speedy, factual, complete, unbiased, reliable information on the activities of the international organizations, using the most up-to-date media of mass communication.

The work and the structure of the Office of Public Information (OPI) are governed by 'Basic Principles Underlying the Public Information Activities of the United Nations', which were adopted by the General Assembly in February 1952. The United Nations Secretariat was instructed that its task of promoting informed understanding of United Nations work and purposes should be carried out mainly by assisting existing official and non-official agencies, by undertaking positive information activities, by supplementing existing services, by not deviating from impartiality and objectivity and by giving special attention to areas where information services are less developed.

In accordance with these principles, OPI in the first place arranges for representatives of information media—the press, radio, films, photographers, NGOs, educational groups—to have access to sources of information. It organizes their admission to United Nations meetings and assists in establishing contacts with delegations and the secretariat. Representatives of all media are provided with complete information and are helped to produce their own information material.

Furthermore, information is disseminated through existing channels. Headquarters and Information Centres send out press material and photographs to news agencies and newspapers; they dispatch live, recorded or written radio material to national broadcasting systems; distribute films through commercial and non-commercial organizations; supply suitable material to educational institutions and NGOs. In short, OPI addresses itself to the general public mainly through 're-dissemination'.

GATHERING OF BASIC MATERIAL

This is, of course, an important function of the information services. It is done principally by the Press, Publications and Public Services Divison of OPI. The editorial services of the division are responsible for the production of the basic written material, issued by OPI for use by accredited correspondents at headquarters, and by others, such as NGOs, who follow the day-to-day activities of the United Nations. This basic material is used by other units of OPI for regional distribution, for publications and for reference.

Information is gathered in the first place from the proceedings of the various organs of the United Nations. Experienced press officers cover meetings and collect information on the results of those sessions which are not open to the press. Their reports, factual and objective, are issued as soon as possible after the close of the meetings. To assist correspondents, many of whom find the United Nations a difficult assignment to cover single-handed, especially at times when several important bodies may be meeting simultaneously; running stories, in the form of 'takes', are issued on the main political meetings (plenaries of the Assembly, the Security Council, the Political Committees of the Assembly).

Reports on the meetings are supplemented by background material, such as annotated agendas and round-ups of the sessions of United Nations bodies. Advance texts are issued whenever possible.

An important source of information are official reports and documents, studies and periodical publications, which are summarized in special press releases. Further information is obtained from the office of the Secretary General and other secretarial departments, from reports by information officers assigned to field missions, from Specialized Agencies and from interviews with technical assistance experts.

All this information goes to the Central Press Desk to be finally edited and issued in the form of press releases.

Information material on the activities of the Specialized Agencies is regularly supplied to United Nations services from the Specialized Agencies headquarters and from the field, and whenever required, is issued in the form of United Nations press releases, which are distributed and processed in the same way as the United Nations' own material.

MATERIAL OF TOPICAL INTEREST

The immense amount of information material provided by the work of the United Nations can be roughly divided into two categories, topical and background.

Material of topical interest covers the deliberations and the decisions of the principal United Nations organs, such as the Security Council and the General Assembly, together with activities in the field in execution of these decisions, such as the establishment and working of observation groups or the action of the United Nations in emergency situations (e.g., the Suez crisis).

These activities, like any other political event of international importance, are reported by correspondents accredited to the United Nations, or by correspondents on the spot. United Nations information services provide facilities for reporting, as well as the basic information, that is, the raw material. When a large-scale meeting, such that of the General Assembly, is being covered, OPI press releases and 'takes' enable a single correspondent to follow a number of meetings without actually taking a seat in the press gallery. In the field, press officers are there to guide the correspondents, to brief them, to facilitate their movements and, occasionally, to issue a 'hand-out'.

BACKGROUND MATERIAL

The other category of United Nations reporting covers a much wider area, and is mainly the job of the working journalist in the editorial office. Towards him are directed the activities of the Information Centres.

Unlike the international agencies and a very few great national dailies, the average newspaper is neither staffed nor equipped to deal with the great mass of material on the United Nations which flows into the editorial offices. It is not easy to select and to edit all that material, or to comment on it. The topical story which the newspaper office receives from an agency or, more rarely, from its correspondent, is ready for insertion. This is not the case with information concerning the work of the specialized organs of the United Nations, or of the Specialized Agencies; nor with information on particular projects and programmes, which are often of vital importance to the area in which the newspaper is published.

The required reference is not very likely to be found in the newspaper's library. Assistance is essential in finding one's way among the mountains of documentation. And the Information Centres with their reference libraries are there to provide guidance in a largely unexplored field.

The United Nations system covers the world and is engaged in activities of vital concern to nations, communities, and the individual. Information of interest to the specialist and to the man in the street alike is provided by these activities. Specialized periodicals, in particular, should be able to find a wealth of most interesting and instructive material in United Nations documentation and reports. The annual economic surveys of the United Nations and other such documents receive a world-wide coverage on the day of publication but this is only a portion of the material available on economic, social and technical assistance problems, as well as on studies and activities of the Specialized Agencies.

The use made of the material provided by the Economic Commission for Europe serves as a good example: agricultural price-trends, coal production and coal export statistics, steel reviews, and similar reports are found by trade and professional publications to be most useful sources of material of great interest and value to the business community.

FACILITIES FOR PRESS CORRESPONDENTS

Bona fide press correspondents, appointed by their agency, newspaper or periodical to cover the activities of the United Nations, are 'accredited' by the respective information services at Headquarters, at the European Office of the United Nations, and at conferences held under the auspices of the United Nations, wherever they take place. An accredited correspondent has free access to all the information sources of the organization and receives, free of charge, the information material issued by United Nations services. He is supplied with a special admission card which enables him to enter and move freely in United Nations buildings, and to use all the facilities provided for correspondents.

These facilities, at Headquarters and in Geneva, include first of all a press working area, situated in close vicinity to United Nations press services. A press room is equipped with all that a correspondent needs: desks with typewriters and telephones, a loudspeaker (which announces events), earphones to enable him to listen in to the principal debates of the day, telephone booths nearby for long-distance calls, offices of wire agencies and teletypes, and, of course, a snack bar. Press agencies and some of the larger dailies have their own offices.

Press releases are made available to the correspondents as soon as they are ready, at the documents desk in the press working area. A document distribution clerk is at the disposal of correspondents whenever they need a specific document. A reference library is there to assist them. Certain press releases are provided with an embargo date and hour, at which they can be used—and there is no greater offence against the professional code than a breach of this embargo.

Releases are issued over a United Nations teletype circuit to a number of newspapers and agencies in New York, which subscribe to the service. Selected releases are also mailed, mainly to specialized and trade papers.

Accreditation of correspondents of all media, which at Headquarters necessitates extensive dealings with United States authorities under the Headquarters agreement, is done in New York by the Press Service, which also arranges all press conferences by delegations and Secretariat officials. These press conferences are, of course, an important addition to other sources of information, and, as a rule, press releases are not issued on them. In the case of the regular press conferences given by the Secretary-General a transcript is issued shortly after the close of the conference.

Press liaison officers provide frequent informal briefings on current subjects, make seating arrangements for meetings, keep correspondents advised on coming events, documents, and releases. Assistance is also provided to delegations in their relations with correpondents, and in the issuing of statements and announcements by delegations.

The Specialized Agencies have similar arrangements for correspondents who are accredited to them.

On an average, 280 press correspondents from some thirty-five countries are accredited on a year-round basis at Headquarters (this figure doubles during the General Assembly), some seventy radio and television correspondents and another hundred newsreelmen and photographers. The European Office carries a hundred names on its list of accredited correspondents.

Accredited correspondents, both at Headquarters and in Geneva, have organized their associations, which are recognized professional representations of the news personnel assigned to cover the United Nations. Lunches of the associations for prominent United Nations personalities often provide a fitting occasion for important pronouncements of topical interest.

SERVICES IN THE FIELD: THE NETWORK OF INFORMATION CENTRES

The establishment of a 'system of Information Centres on an adequate regional and/or linguistic basis with due regard to actual varying needs' has been placed high on the list of the recommendations and the basic principles which constitute the mandate of OPI. At present, 27 Information Centres and offices cover 83 countries and territories, in all five continents.

The essential job of an Information Centre is to meet the need for information about the United Nations system in its area. This is done through day-to-day contacts on the spot and by regularly supplying information material in the idiom of the country, adapted to the information needs and techniques of the region.

The material which OPI supplies to the centres is substantially the same for all, but with emphasis on regional interest.

The centres are the distributors of all United Nations material in their areas for the press, for radio and television services, publications, films, filmstrips, photos, posters. Their advice and co-operation are indispensable in selecting, translating and adapting the material to be used in the field. Several centres issue information bulletins in the languages of their areas. Small reference libraries are an essential part of the centres' services.

A plentiful supply of well-selected and well-adapted material for regional use is of particular importance in countries less developed on the information side, which rely to a very large extent on the centres for information on the United Nations for all media.

Particular stress is laid by the centres on services for the NGOs and educational institutions, which address themselves to the centres not only for information but also for guidance in their work of disseminating knowledge of, or teaching about, the United Nations.

Also, in several countries where the centres are the only United Nations offices, they inevitably have to perform duties not directly concerned with information.

OPI PUBLICATIONS

More than 12 million copies of periodicals, reference books, pamphlets and leaflets—some of them in as many as 37 languages—have been issued by OPI since 1946, and distributed throughout the world. The Human Rights Declaration was published in 50 languages.

The principal periodical is the *United Nations Review*, published in New York, a monthly magazine intended to give a concise account of the activities of the United Nations and its related agencies. Apart from satisfying the interest of the general public for comprehensive information about the United Nations, it is of great assistance to writers, editorialists, commentators, teachers and students of international affairs. A monthly *Revue des Nations Unies* is published in Paris, edited and produced in a way to suit the reading habits of French-speaking people. A Spanish language edition, *Revista de las Naciones Unidas* is published monthly from Mexico City. Certain articles from the *Review* are reprinted in pamphlet form.

United Nations services prepare the material for the *Yearbook* of the United Nations, which is published by the Columbia University Press in New York. This volume, comprising several hundred pages, appears towards the end of each year, reviewing the work of the United Nations system for the preceding 12 months. It is a running history of the United Nations, an indispensable work of reference and research.

A general reference publication, *Everyman's United Nations*, reprinted and brought up to date every two to three years, is supplemented by pamphlets on specific activities of various United Nations organs, and by short, concise, factual leaflets on many subjects.

The bulk of OPI publications consists of popular brochures and leaflets of a general nature on the United Nations—such as *Basic Facts about the UN, The UN in Brief,* or on special subjects, e.g., *Pooling Skills for Human Progress* (on technical assistance), *A Sacred Trust* (the work for dependent peoples), *Our Rights as Human Beings,* etc.

RADIO

The primary duty of the Radio Division of OPI is to provide services for the broadcasting systems of Member States, non-member countries and territories. These services include transmitting and recording facilities for accredited radio correspondents who cover the United Nations at New York and in Geneva, and—whenever practicable—in the course of major meetings in the field. United Nations radio studios in New York and in Geneva are at the disposal of accredited radio correspondents for direct broadcast or for recording information on the United Nations.

The United Nations radio produces its own news and information programmes about day-to-day developments: meetings and field activities, the work of the Specialized Agencies, delegates' statements on matters concerning the United Nations. Live transmission of debates is arranged on major occasions. United Nations radio reporters cover major events in the field and provide valuable material for feature and documentary programmes. These programmes are regularly re-broadcast on national wave-lengths to home audiences in more than 50 Member States and more than 40 non-Member States and territories.

Normally, news and feature programmes in other than the five official languages are undertaken only in co-operation with the national radio systems and when the station network concerned is able to re-broadcast them.

During the non-Assembly period, emphasis is laid on programmes of broad educational value, on features, and documentary programmes. Many of these programmes are produced locally, by radio officers assigned to larger Information Centres, which maintain close working contacts with national systems. Emphasis is laid on services to countries with limited national resources in the field of information.

TELEVISION

United Nations television services have developed rapidly. Facilities are provided to national television systems in the form of programmes dispatched directly from the United Nations. Filmed news which highlights major events is thus supplied to many TV networks.

United Nations television is producing its own features and has contracts with several major general television and educational networks for the supply and use of its material. United Nations films are also often used by national networks.

FILMS

A considerable number of films illustrating various United Nations activities and depicting subjects of international action are now available to the public all over the world. United Nations services have produced a great many films, and have promoted the production by film and newsreel companies of many more.

The principal task of United Nations film services is, indeed, to maintain contact, at headquarters and in the field through the Information Centres, with film producers, providing facilities and advice, sometimes material. Outside production is stimulated by suggesting suitable subjects, by guidance on scripts, by supplying documentation and material from the United Nations Film Footage Library and, if necessary, film raw stock. The United Nations film library now contains some 3 million feet of historical records, available at laboratory costs to external producers. The library is constantly replenished by material from the United Nations' own cameramen who film United Nations events, and by footage on the United Nations acquired from outside cameramen. The catalogue of the library is available to interested producers.

Several newsreel companies with world-wide distribution systems have their correspondents accredited to the United Nations.

The United Nations' own production of films is now concentrated on short documentary films on the activities of the United Nations family as a whole. Language versions are made to ensure the widest distribution, especially in underdeveloped areas. The average length of a United Nations film is from 10 to 30 minutes. One feature-length documentary in Eastman colour, of 90 minutes duration, has also been produced (*Power among Men*).

The pattern of distribution of United Nations films is flexible and varies from country to country, especially in underdeveloped areas. Contracts in force in a number of countries permit the showing of United Nations films in cinemas through commercial theatrical circuits, but a much larger public is reached through non-theatrical distribution. NGOs, schools, clubs, churches, whoever is interested in showing United Nations films can obtain them from the nearest Information Centre or from other authorized sources free of charge or at a nominal cost.

FILMSTRIPS

Several filmstrips are produced each year, mainly for use in schools and by NGOs. They depict basic and current United Nations activities. Dupe negatives are available for reprint by interested national producers with texts adapted to the requirements of the country or region concerned.

PHOTOS AND EXHIBITS

United Nations still photos are available from Headquarters and through Information Centres, which are supplied with material of regional interest. The United Nations Photo Library in New York has more than 63,000 selected negatives of United Nations events and personalities. A large photo library has been organized in Geneva and others have been formed on a continental scale.

Photographic coverage of United Nations and Specialized Agencies activities is provided by staff photographers who are either at Headquarters or attached to Information Centres or missions, and by free-lance photographers trained for United Nations work.

Photo catalogues with prototypes of new acquisitions are circulated to agencies and newspapers, to assist them in ordering the glossy prints they intend to use. Photo features on various subjects are also available.

Wall sheets, a photo reportage of about ten pictures on specific subjects, are made mainly for use in schools, in meeting-houses, etc. These are also valuable elements in exhibitions on United Nations subjects. United Nations services can on occasions supply small exhibitions consisting of a number of sheets with enlarged photos and texts. These can be had from Information Centres.

EDUCATION AND TEACHING ABOUT THE UNITED NATIONS

Member States have undertaken in a General Assembly resolution to include 'Teaching about the United Nations' in the curricula of their school systems. Unesco and the United Nations co-operate in assisting the governments and the educational authorities to carry out programmes of teaching about international action. Basic teaching material is produced, general information material is adapted to suit educational purposes and, principally, advice and assistance are rendered in the national production of textbooks and other teaching material about the United Nations system.

A network of some 600 volunteer educational units in 90 countries has been organized to stimulate interest and to act as a source of information on the United Nations in colleges and schools. These units receive material and advice from the educational section of OPI.

Interne programmes are organized regularly at Headquarters for students. Details of these programmes can be had from Information Centres. Special courses and seminars can be organized for schools and students groups at headquarters and in Geneva, or in any other regional

193

office. Conducted educational tours of United Nations buildings in New York and in Geneva are free of charge.

Services for NGOs which form an important part of the activities of the OPI are described in the course on relations with the NGOs.[1]

INFORMATION SERVICES OF THE SPECIALIZED AGENCIES

The major Agencies have their own public information services organized on patterns similar to those of the United Nations. The information material produced by the Agencies is available directly from them or through United Nations information services and Information Centres.

Co-ordination and liaison in the field of public information between the United Nations and Specialized Agencies is effected through the Consultative Committee on Public Information (CCPI). Members of CCPI are OPI and the information services of nine Agencies. The committee discusses matters of information policies and progress of co-operation. It is not an operating body, but several joint operations have been organized and executed under its auspices, notably on technical assistance. The CCPI work of co-ordination is aimed mainly at avoiding duplication of activities.

ILO, FAO, Unesco and WHO maintain information liaison officers at United Nations Headquarters. The Information Centres serve as regional liaison offices where the Agencies are engaged in information activities.

REVIEW OF THE WORK OF UNITED NATIONS INFORMATION SERVICES

At its 1957 session the General Assembly decided to establish a six-member expert committee to review and to appraise the work, methods, and effectiveness of the United Nations public information services, with the purpose of assuring maximum efficiency with minimum expenditure.

The committee's report laid stress on work in the field, mainly through the network of Information Centres. At the 1959 session of the General Assembly, following a debate in the Fifth Committee on the execution by the Secretariat of the experts' recommendations, a resolution was adopted asking, among other things, for the creation of new centres in areas with insufficiently developed information media.

---

1. See page 109.

Appendixes

Country	United Nations	IAEA	ILO	FAO	Unesco [2]	WHO [3]	BANK FUND	IFC	ICAO	UPU [4]	ITU [5]	WMO [6]	IMCO [7]
Afghanistan	×	×	×	×	×	×	×	×	×	×	×	×	—
Albania.	×	×	×	—	×	×	—	—	—	×	×	×	—
Argentina.	×	×	×	×	×	×	×	×	×	×	×	×	×
Australia	×	×	×	×	×	×	×	×	×	×	×	×	×
Austria	×	×	×	×	×	×	×	×	×	×	×	×	—
Belgium.	×	×	×	×	×	×	×	×	×	×	×	×	×
Bolivia	×	—	×	×	×	×	×	×	×	×	×	×	—
Brazil.	×	×	×	×	×	×	×	×	×	×	×	×	—
Bulgaria	×	×	×	—	×	×	—	—	—	×	×	×	×
Burma	×	×	×	×	×	×	×	×	×	×	×	×	×
Byelorussian SSR . .	×	×	×	—	×	×	—	—	—	×	×	×	—
Cambodia.	×	×	—	×	×	×	—	—	×	×	×	×	—
Cameroun.	×	—	×	×	×	×	—	—	×	×	—	×	—
Canada.	×	×	×	×	×	×	×	×	×	×	×	×	×
Central African Republic. .	×	—	×	—	×	×	—	—	—	—	×	—	—
Ceylon	×	×	×	×	×	×	×	×	×	×	×	×	—
Chad.	×	—	×	—	—	—	—	—	—	—	×	—	—
Chile.	×	×	×	×	×	×	×	×	×	×	×	×	—
China	×	×	×	—	×	×	×	—	×	×	×	×	×
Colombia	×	×	×	×	×	×	×	×	×	×	×	—	—
Congo (Brazzaville) .	×	—	×	—	×	×	—	—	—	×	×	—	—
Congo (Léopoldville) .	×	—	×	—	×	—	—	—	—	—	—	×	—
Costa Rica	×	—	×	×	×	×	×	×	×	×	×	—	—
Cuba.	×	×	×	×	×	×	—[8]	—	×	×	×	×	—
Cyprus	×	—	×	×	—	—	—	—	—	—	—	—	—
Czechoslovakia . . .	×	×	×	—	×	×	—	—	×	×	×	×	—
Dahomey.	×	—	—	—	×	×	—	—	—	—	—	—	—
Denmark	×	×	×	×	×	×	×	×	×	×	×	×	×
Dominican Republic .	×	×	×	×	×	×	—[8]	—	×	×	×	×	×
Ecuador	×	×	×	×	×	×	×	×	×	×	×	×	×
El Salvador	×	×	×	×	×	×	×	×	×	×	×	×	—
Ethiopia	×	×	×	×	×	×	×	×	×	×	×	×	—
Finland.	×	×	×	×	×	×	×	×	×	×	×	×	×
France	×	×	×	×	×	×	×	×	×	×	×	×	×
Gabon	×	—	×	—	×	×	—	—	—	—	—	—	—
Federal Republic of Germany	—	×	×	×	×	×	×	×	×	×	×	×	×

Country	United Nations	IAEA	ILO	FAO	Unesco [2]	WHO [3]	BANK FUND	IFC	ICAO	UPU [4]	ITU [5]	WMO [6]	IMCO [7]
Ghana	×	×	×	×	×	×	×	×	×	×	×	×	×
Greece	×	×	×	×	×	×	×	×	×	×	×	×	×
Guatemala	×	×	×	×	×	×	×	×	×	×	×	×	—
Guinea	×	—	×	×	×	×	—	—	×	×	×	×	—
Haiti	×	×	×	×	×	×	×	×	×	×	×	×	×
Holy See	—	×	—	—	—	—	—	—	—	×	×	—	—
Honduras	×	×	×	×	×	×	×	×	×	×	×	×	×
Hungary	×	×	×	—	×	×	—	—	—	×	×	×	—
Iceland	×	×	×	×	—	×	×	×	×	×	×	×	×
India	×	×	×	×	×	×	×	×	×	×	×	×	×
Indonesia	×	×	×	×	×	×	×	×	×	×	×	×	—
Iran	×	×	×	×	×	×	×	×	×	×	×	×	×
Iraq	×	×	×	×	×	×	×	×	×	×	×	×	—
Ireland	×	—	×	×	—	×	×	×	×	×	×	×	×
Israel	×	×	×	×	×	×	×	×	×	×	×	×	×
Italy	×	×	×	×	×	×	×	×	×	×	×	×	×
Ivory Coast	×	—	×	—	×	—	—	—	×	—	—	×	×
Japan	×	×	×	×	×	×	×	×	×	×	×	×	×
Jordan	×	—	×	×	×	×	×	×	×	×	×	×	—
Korea (Republic of)	—	×	—	×	×	×	×	—	×	×	×	×	—
Kuwait	—	—	—	—	×	—	×	—	×	×	×	—	×
Laos	×	—	—	×	×	×	—	—	×	×	×	×	—
Lebanon	×	—	×	×	×	×	×	×	×	×	×	×	—
Liberia	×	—	×	×	×	×	—	—	×	×	×	—	×
Libya	×	—	×	×	×	×	×	×	×	×	×	×	—
Luxembourg	×	×	×	×	×	×	×	×	×	×	×	×	—
Madagascar	×	—	×	—	×	—	—	—	—	—	—	×	—
Malaya (Federation of)	×	—	×	×	×	×	×	×	×	×	×	×	—
Mali	×	—	×	—	×	×	—	—	—	—	×	×	—
Mexico	×	×	×	×	×	×	×	×	×	×	×	×	×
Monaco	—	×	—	—	×	×	—	—	—	×	×	×	—
Morocco	×	×	×	×	×	×	×	—	×	×	×	×	—
Nepal	×	—	—	×	×	×	—	—	×	×	×	—	—
Netherlands	×	×	×	×	×	×	×	×	×	×	×	×	×
New Zealand	×	×	×	×	×	×	—	—	×	×	×	×	×
Nicaragua	×	×	×	×	×	×	×	×	×	×	×	×	—
Niger	×	—	—	—	×	×	—	—	—	—	×	×	—
Nigeria	×	—	×	×	×	×	—	—	—	—	—	—	—
Norway	×	×	×	×	×	×	×	×	×	×	×	×	×
Pakistan	×	×	×	×	×	×	×	×	×	×	×	×	×
Panama	×	—	×	×	×	×	×	×	×	×	×	—	×
Paraguay	×	×	×	×	×	×	×	×	×	×	×	×	—
Peru	×	×	×	×	×	×	×	×	×	×	×	×	—
Philippines	×	×	×	×	×	×	×	×	×	×	×	×	—
Poland	×	×	×	×	×	×	—	—	×	×	×	×	×

Country	United Nations	IAEA	ILO	FAO	Unesco[2]	WHO[3]	BANK FUND	IFC	ICAO	UPU[4]	ITU[5]	WMO[6]	IMCO[7]
Portugal	×	×	×	×	—	×	—	—	×	×	×	×	—
Rumania	×	×	×	—	×	×	—	—	—	×	×	×	—
San Marino	—	—	—	—	—	—	—	—	—	×	—	—	—
Saudi Arabia	×	—	—	×	×	×	×	—	—	×	×	×	—
Senegal	×	—	×	—	×	×	—	—	—	—	×	×	×
Somalia	×	—	×	—	×	—	—	—	—	×	—	×	×
Spain	×	×	×	×	×	×	×	×	×	×	×	×	—
Sudan	×	×	×	×	×	×	×	×	×	×	×	×	—
Sweden	×	×	×	×	×	×	×	×	×	×	×	×	×
Switzerland	—	×	×	×	×	×	—	—	×	×	×	×	×
Thailand	×	×	×	×	×	×	×	×	×	×	×	×	—
Togo	×	—	×	×	×	×	—	—	—	—	×	×	—
Tunisia	×	×	×	×	×	×	×	—	×	×	×	×	—
Turkey	×	×	×	×	×	×	×	×	×	×	×	×	×
Ukrainian SSR	×	×	×	—	×	×	—	—	—	×	×	×	—
Union of South Africa	×	×	×	×	—	×	×	×	×	×	×	×	—
Union of Soviet Socialist Republics	×	×	×	—	×	×	—	—	—	×	×	×	×
United Arab Republic	×	×	×	×	×	×	×	×	×	×	×	×	×
United Kingdom	×	×	×	×	×	×	×	×	×	×	×	×	×
United States of America	×	×	×	×	×	×	×	×	×	×	×	×	×
Upper Volta	×	—	×	—	×	×	—	—	—	—	×	×	—
Uruguay	×	—	×	×	×	×	—	—	×	×	×	×	—
Venezuela	×	×	×	×	×	×	×	—	×	×	×	×	×
Vietnam	—	×	×	×	×	×	—	—	×	×	×	×	×
Yemen	×	—	—	×	—	×	—	—	—	×	×	—	—
Yugoslavia	×	×	×	×	×	×	×	—	×	×	×	×	×
Total members	99	73	95	81	98	100	66	58	80	100	101	108	43
Date on which total was compiled	7/10/ 1960	31/10/ 1960	21/11/ 1960	7/11/ 1960	3/12/ 1960	28/11/ 1960	3/12/ 1960	3/12/ 1960	30/11/ 1960	1/12/ 1960	12/12/ 1960	11/12/ 1960	17/11/ 1960

1. Designations are as given by each Agency; for some members designations are in the process of change.
2. Unesco has six associate members: Singapore, Sierra Leone, Ruanda-Urundi, Tanganyika, Mauritius and Federation of the West Indies.
3. WHO has three associate members: Cyprus, Federation of Rhodesia and Nyasaland, and Sierra Leone.
4. UPU members also include Algeria; Netherlands Antilles and Surinam; Portuguese provinces in West Africa; Portuguese provinces in East Africa, Asia and Oceania; Spanish territories in Africa; whole of the territories represented by the French Office of Overseas Posts and Telecommunications; whole of the British Overseas Territories, etc.; whole of the territories of whole of the British Overseas Teritoires, etc.; whole of the territories of the United States of America, including the Trust Territory of the Pacific Islands.
5. In ITU, Union of South Africa membership includes Territory of South

West Africa; ITU members also include overseas States of the French Community and French overseas territories; Spanish provinces in Africa; Portuguese overseas provinces; Federation of Rhodesia and Nyasaland; territories of the United States of America; and overseas territories for the international relations of which the government of the United Kingdom of Great Britain and Northern Ireland is responsible.

ITU also has five associate members: British East Africa, British West Africa, Bermuda-British Caribbean Group, Singapore-British Borneo Group, and Somaliland.

6. WMO members also include: British East African Territories, including the Seychelles; British West African Territories; Federation of Rhodesia and Nyasaland; States of the French Community in Equatorial Africa; French Oceania; States of the French Community in West Africa; Hong Kong; Mauritius; Netherlands Antilles; Netherlands New Guinea; New Caledonia; Portuguese East Africa; Portuguese West Africa; Ruanda-Urundi; Singapore and the British Territories in Borneo; Spanish Guinea Territories; Surinam; the West Indies, Bahamas, British Guinea, British Honduras, and the Virgin Islands.

7. IMCO has one associate member: Nigeria.
8. Member of FUND but not of BANK.

II. LIST OF MEMBERS OF THE UNITED NATIONS FAMILY OF INTERGOVERNMENTAL ORGANIZATIONS

United Nations, New York. Secretary General: Dag Hammarskjøld (Sweden).

International Labour Organisation (ILO), Geneva. Director-General: David A. Morse (United States).

Food and Agriculture Organization of the United Nations (FAO), Rome. Director-General: B. R. Sen (India).

United Nations Educational, Scientific and Cultural Organization (Unesco), Paris. Director-General: Vittorino Veronese (Italy).

World Health Organization (WHO), Geneva. Director-General: Dr. M. G. Candau (Brazil).

International Bank for Reconstruction and Development (BANK), Washington. President: Eugene R. Black (United States).

International Finance Corporation (IFC), Washington. President: Robert L. Garner (United States).

International Monetary Fund (FUND), Washington. Managing Director: Per Jacobson (Sweden).

International Civil Aviation Organization (ICAO), Montreal. Secretary-General: Ronald M. Macdonnel (Canada).

Universal Postal Union (UPU), Berne. Director: Dr. Fritz Hess (Switzerland).

International Telecommunication Union (ITU), Geneva. Acting Secretary-General: Gerald C. Gross (United States).

World Meteorological Organization (WMO), Geneva. Secretary-General: David A. Davies (United Kingdom).

Intergovernmental Maritime Consultative Organization (IMCO), London. Secretary-General: Ove Nielsen (Denmark).

International Atomic Energy Agency (IAEA), Vienna. Director-General: Sterling Cole (United States).

General Agreement on Tariffs and Trade (GATT), Geneva. Executive Secretary: Wyndham White (United Kingdom).

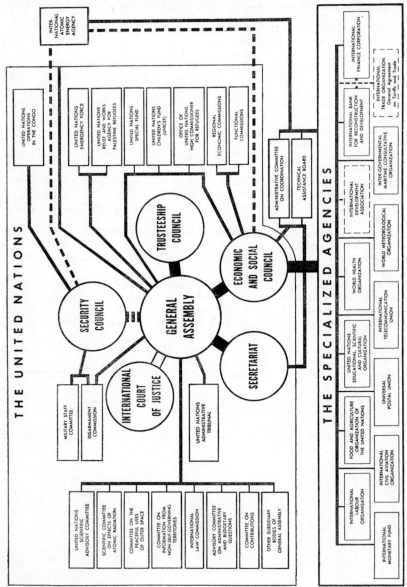

IV. MEMBERSHIP OF PRINCIPAL ORGANS
OF THE UNITED NATIONS

Permanent members: China, France, the USSR, the United Kingdom and the United States.

Non-permanent members: Argentina, Italy, Poland,[1] Tunisia (until 1961), Ceylon, Ecuador (until 1962).

ECONOMIC AND SOCIAL COUNCIL [2]

Afghanistan	(1962)	Denmark	(1963)	Spain	(1962)
Brazil	(1963)	France	(1961)	Sudan	(1961)
Bulgaria	(1962)	Japan	(1963)	USSR	(1963)
Chile	(1961)	Netherlands	(1961)	United Kingdom	(1963)
China	(1961)	New Zealand	(1962)	United States	(1962)
Costa Rica	(1961)	Poland	(1963)	Venezuela	(1962)

TRUSTEESHIP COUNCIL

Countries administering trust territories: Australia, Belgium, France, Italy, New Zealand, United Kingdom, United States.

Permanent members of the Security Council not administering trust territories: China, Union of Soviet Socialist Republics.

Countries not administering trust territories elected by the General Assembly: Burma, Paraguay, United Arab Republic (until 1962) and Bolivia and India (until 1963).

---

1. After a series of inconclusive ballots at the 1959 Assembly in which Poland and Turkey failed to secure the requisite two-thirds majority for election to the Security Council, the President of the General Assembly announced before the last ballot an understanding whereby Poland would be the sole candidate and, if elected, she would serve on the Council for the calendar year 1960 and her resignation would become effective 31 December 1960. During the fifteenth session of the Assembly, Turkey would be the sole candidate to fill the vacancy thus created and would serve on the Council for the year 1961.
2. Date of resignation shown in parentheses.

INTERNATIONAL COURT OF JUSTICE [1]

Ricardo J. Alfaro (Panama) (1964).
E. C. Armand-Ugon (Uruguay) (1961).
Abdel Hamid Badawi (United Arab Republic) (1967).
Jules Basdevant (France) (1964).
Roberto Cordova (Mexico) (1964).
Green H. Hackworth (United States) (1961).
Helge Klaested (President) (Norway) (1961).
Feodor Ivanovich Kojevnikov (USSR) (1961).
V. K. Wellington Koo (China) (1967).
Hersch Lauterpacht (United Kingdom) (1964).
Lucio M. Moreno Quintana (Argentina) (1964.)
Sir Percy Spender (Australia) (1967).
Jean Spiropoulos (Greece) (1967).
Bohdan Winiarski (Poland) (1967).
Muhammad Zafrulla Khan (Pakistan) (1961).

---

1. Date of expiration of term of office shown in parentheses. All terms expire on 5 February of the year designated.

V. COMMISSIONS, COMMITTEES AND AGENCIES OF THE UNITED NATIONS

Advisory Committee on Administrative and Budgetary Questions, United Nations, New York. Chairman: Thanassis Aghnides (Greece).

Economic Commission for Africa (ECA), Addis Ababa. Executive Secretary: Mekki Abbas (Sudan).

Economic Commission for Asia and the Far East (ECAFE), Bangkok. Executive Secretary: U Nyun (Burma).

Economic Commission for Europe (ECE), Geneva. Executive Secretary: Sakari Tuomioja (Finland).

Economic Commission for Latin America (ECLA), Santiago. Executive Secretary: Raoul Prebisch (Argentina).

International Law Commission (ILC) (21 members).

United Nations Conciliation Commission for Palestine.

United Nations Commission for the Unification and Rehabilitation of Korea, (UNCURK), Seoul.

United Nations Emergency Force (UNEF), Gaza. Chief of Staff: Major General P. S. Gyani (India).

United Nations High Commissioner for Refugees (UNREF), Geneva. High Commissioner: Dr. Auguste R. Lindt (Switzerland).

United Nations Relief and Works Agency for Palestine Refugees (UNWRA), Beirut. Director: J. H. Davis (United States).

United Nations Truce and Supervision Organization (UNTSO), Jerusalem. Chief of Staff: Major General Carl von Horn (Sweden).

VI. PRINCIPAL OFFICERS OF THE SECRETARIAT OF THE UNITED NATIONS

Secretary-General: Dag Hammarskjøld (Sweden).
Executive Assistant to the Secretary-General: Andrew W. Cordier (United States).
Legal Counsel: Constantin Stavropoulos (Greece).
Controller: Bruce R. Turner (New Zealand).
Director of Personnel: W. A. B. Hamilton (United Kingdom).
Under-Secretary for Special Political Affairs: Ralph J. Bunche (United States).
Under-Secretary for Special Political Affairs: C. V. Narasimhan (India).
Under-Secretary for Political and Security Council Affairs (vacant).
Under-Secretary for Economic and Social Affairs: Philippe de Seynes (France).
Commissioner for Technical Assistance: Roberto M. Heurtematte (Panama).
Managing Director of the United Nations Special Fund: Paul Hoffman (United States).
Under-Secretary for Trusteeship and Information from Non-self-governing Territories: Dragoslav Protitch (Yugoslavia).
Office of Public Information. Acting Head: Alfred G. Katzin (Union of South Africa).
Under-Secretary for Conference Services: Victor A. Hoo (China).
Director of General Services: David B. Vaughan (United States).
Executive Director of the United Nations Children's Fund (Unicef): Maurice Pate (United States).
Executive Chairman of the Technical Assistance Board: David Owen (United Kingdom).
Director of the United Nations European Office: P. P. Spinelli (Italy).
United Nations High Commissioner for Refugees: Auguste Lindt (Switzerland).
Director of the United Nations Relief and Works Agency for Palestine Refugees in the Near East: John H. Davis (United States).
Economic Commission for Europe. Executive Secretary: Sakari Tuomioja (Finland).
Economic Commission for Asia and the Far East. Executive Secretary: U Nyun (Burma).
Economic Commission for Latin America. Executive Secretary: Raul Prebisch (Argentina).
Economic Commission for Africa. Executive Secretary: Mekki Abbas (Sudan).

VII. UNITED NATIONS INFORMATION CENTRES AND OFFICES

Accra, Ghana. Covering Gambia, Ghana, Nigeria, Sierra Leone.

Addis Ababa, Ethiopia. ECA Information Officer, Ethiopia.

Athens, Greece. Covering Greece, Israel and Turkey.

Bangkok, Thailand. ECAFE Information Officer, covering Cambodia, Laos, Thailand, Federation of Malaya and Singapore, Viet-Nam.

Belgrade, Yugoslavia. Covering Albania and Yugoslavia.

Bogota, Colombia. Covering Colombia, Ecuador, Venezuela.

Buenos Aires, Argentina. Covering Argentina, Paraguay, Uruguay.

Cairo, United Arab Republic (Egypt). Covering Iraq, Jordan, Lebanon, Libya, Saudi Arabia, Sudan, United Arab Republic, Yemen.

Copenhagen, Denmark. Covering Denmark, Finland, Iceland, Norway, Sweden.

Djakarta, Indonesia. Information Officer for Indonesia.

Geneva, Switzerland. Information Service of the European Office, covering Austria, Bulgaria, Germany, Hungary, Poland, Rumania, Switzerland.

Kabul, Afghanistan. Covering Afghanistan.

Karachi, Pakistan. Covering Pakistan.

Lima, Peru. Covering Bolivia, Peru.

London, United Kingdom. Covering Ireland, Netherlands, United Kingdom.

Manila, Philippines. Covering the Philippines.

Mexico City, Mexico. Covering Costa Rica, Cuba, Dominican Republic, El Salvador, Guatemala, Honduras, Mexico, Nicaragua, Panama.

Moscow, USSR. Covering Byelorussian SSR, Ukrainian SSR, USSR.

New Delhi, India. Covering Ceylon, India, Nepal.

Paris, France. Covering Belgium, France, Luxembourg.

Prague, Czechoslovakia. Covering Czechoslovakia.

Rangoon, Burma. Covering Burma.

Rio de Janeiro, Brazil. Covering Brazil.

Rome, Italy. Covering Italy.

Santiago, Chile. ECLA Information Officer.

Sydney, Australia. Covering Australia, New Zealand.

Teheran, Iran. Covering Iran.

Tokyo, Japan. Covering Japan.

Washington, United States of America.

VIII. ABBREVIATIONS

ACC	Administrative Committee on Co-ordination of the United Nations and the Specialized Agencies.
ASFEC	Arab States Fundamental Education Centre.
BANK	International Bank for Reconstruction and Development.
CCEP	Consultative Commission for Postal Studies.
CCIs	International Consultative Committees.
CCIR	International Radio Consultative Committee.
CCITT	International Telegraph and Telephone Consultative Committee.
CCPI	Consultative Committee for Public Information.
CERN	European Organization for Nuclear Research.
CIESPAL	International Centre for High Studies in Journalism in Latin America.
CIM	International Music Council.
CIPHS	International Council for Philosophy and Humanistic Studies.
CREFAL	Regional Fundamental Education Centre for Community Development for Latin America.
DSB	Drug Supervisory Body.
ECA	Economic Commission for Africa.
ECAFE	Economic Commission for Asia and the Far East.
ECE	Economic Commission for Europe.
ECLA	Economic Commission for Latin America.
Ecosoc	Economic and Social Council.
FAO	Food and Agriculture Organization of the United Nations.
FICSA	Federation of International Civil Servants' Associations.
FUND	International Monetary Fund.
GA	General Assembly of the United Nations.
GATT	General Agreement on Tariffs and Trade.
IAEA	International Atomic Energy Agency.
IBE	International Bureau of Education.
IAMCR	International Association for Mass Communication Research.
IAPA	International Association of Plastic Arts.
ICAO	International Civil Aviation Organization.
ICEM	Intergovernmental Committee for European Migration.
ICFC	International Centre of Films for Children.
ICJ	International Court of Justice.
ICOM	International Council of Museums.
IFC	International Finance Corporation.
IFLA	International Federation of Library Associations.
IFRB	International Frequency Registration Board.
IFTC	International Film and Television Council.
IGY	International Geophysical Year.
ILC	International Law Commission.

ILO	International Labour Organisation.
IMCO	Intergovernmental Maritime Consultative Organization.
INTERPOL	International Criminal Police Organization.
IRO	International Refugee Organization.
ITI	International Theatre Institute.
ITO	International Trade Organization.
ITU	International Telecommunication Union.
IUA	International Union of Architects.
NGO	Non-governmental organization.
OAS	Organization of American States.
OPEX	Office for the Provision of Operational and Executive Personnel.
OPI	Office of Public Information of the United Nations.
OTC	Organization for Trade Co-operation.
PCOB	Permanent Central Opium Board.
PEN	International PEN Club.
SUNFED	Special United Nations Fund for Economic Development.
TAB	Technical Assistance Board.
TAC	Technical Assistance Committee.
UNAs	United Nations Associations.
UNCCP	United Nations Conciliation Commission for Palestine.
UNCURK	United Nations Commission for the Unification and Rehabilitation of Korea.
UNEF	United Nations Emergency Force.
Unesco	United Nations Educational Scientific and Cultural Organization.
UNHCR	United Nations High Commissioner for Refugees.
Unicef	United Nations Children's Fund.
UNKRA	United Nations Korean Reconstruction Agency.
UNREF	United Nations Refugee Fund.
UNRRA	United Nations Relief and Rehabilitation Administration.
UNRWA	United Nations Relief and Works Agency for Palestine Refugees in the Middle East.
UNTSO	United Nations Truce Supervision Organization.
UPU	Universal Postal Union.
WFUNA	World Federation of United Nations Associations.
WHO	World Health Organization.
WMO	World Meteorological Organization.

Index

211

229